Life in
Spite of
Everything

Life in Spite of Everything

Tales from the Ukrainian East

Victoria Donovan

First published in the United Kingdom in 2025 by
Daunt Books
83 Marylebone High Street
London W1U 4QW
publishing@dauntbooks.co.uk

1

Maps © Thomas Bohm, User Design, Illustration and Typesetting, UK

A CIP catalogue record for this title is available from the British Library

ISBN 978-1-917092-14-2

Typeset by Marsha Swan
Printed and bound in the United Kingdom by Clays Ltd, Elcograf S.p.A.

www.dauntbookspublishing.co.uk

Contents

Line of contact between government controlled and non-government controlled Donbas before February 2022

Preface

I first visited the Ukrainian east, often referred to as Donbas, in the summer of 2019. I was travelling to the chemical-making city of Sievierodonetsk for a summer school that I'd helped to organise, and was taking the overnight train from Kyiv to the nearest railway station in the east in Lysychansk. On boarding the train, I found that I was sharing a cabin with two women from what was already terrorist-occupied Luhansk. The women insisted that I have a glass of the brandy they'd brought along for the journey. They'd had a couple of drinks already and talked loudly over each other for my benefit about how good life was in the occupied zone. 'There are traffic jams everywhere,' one told me, painting the city as a populated and thriving urban metropolis, 'the cinemas are full every night.' I excused myself after a while and went down the train in search of my friend Dima, whose family had been displaced from Luhansk five years earlier, when Russian military and fighting groups had invaded the region. Dima listened to my anecdote about the tipsy women in silence. Then he told me that he sometimes dreamed of his family home in the occupied city, and of the now surely overgrown basketball hoop in his backyard, where he had played as a child.

When I woke the next morning, the skyline, visible through the crack in the blind, was distinctively flat. I went out into the corridor, where Dima and a couple of others in our party were already up, to get a better view of the steppe landscape. The region's iconic coal slag heaps, known as *terykony* in Ukrainian, from the French *terricones*, whizzed regularly past the window. I asked Dima if he'd ever climbed any of these industrial pyramids. 'Of course,' he answered, 'everybody who grew up here has. We can climb one together if you like.' I would climb my first *terykon* in Myrnohrad two years later in July 2021. On the outskirts of this coal-mining 'monotown' (a single-industry settlement of around 50,000 people), I scrambled up the side of a slag heap behind Dima, gripping branches of trees as the shale slipped underfoot. At the top a picturesque view greeted us: a low slice of ebbing sunlight at the horizon, punctuated by more *terykony* and warm yellow streetlamps. At that same moment, Russia was massing thousands of troops and military equipment on the border with Ukraine. Six months later, they would invade and the region would be engulfed by the devastating war that remains ongoing at the time of writing.

People have written about how war erases not only buildings and infrastructures, but a sense of self and professional identity as well.[1] As a researcher who writes about Ukraine but

has no family in the country, I am undoubtedly at the outer limit of this war's emotional orbit, yet nonetheless also experienced a sense of erasure. When Russia invaded, I was in the middle of writing a very different book to this one, about the region known as Donbas, a heavily industrialised and, since 2014, war-impacted part of the Ukrainian east. The book was a more conventional history, written in a detached academic voice, which I'd tried to keep untainted by my feelings of anger and injustice about the structural violences that had caused so much human and environmental suffering to this place and other resource-rich regions like it. The book lingers unfinished in a folder on my desktop. Since Russia launched its full-scale war, I haven't been able to access that detached academic voice to finish it off. Instead, the anger and sadness has poured over onto the pages of my writing. This angry, sad history of Donbas is what you hold in your hands now. It is, it seems, the only story that I am able to write.

My research on Donbas began in my hometown of Cardiff back in 2015. I had been pondering for some time the strange parallels between Wales and Ukraine – the regionalised industrialisation, language politics, and culturally dominant eastern neighbour – and had been lightly googling this topic when I came upon the Hughesovka Research Archive, housed within the city's Glamorgan Archives. This collection documents a chapter in Wales's history about which I then had no idea. It records the migration in the late nineteenth century of hundreds of Welsh miners, engineers, and chemists to a newly founded settlement in what is now Donbas called Hughesovka (named after John Hughes, an industrial entrepreneur from Merthyr Tydfil), then part of the Russian Empire. The Welsh labour migrants stayed in Hughesovka until 1917, when, following the Bolshevik Revolution, the mines they owned and managed were nationalised and they were thrown out of the communist state. Hughesovka became Stalino, named in honour of the dictatorial architect of Soviet industrialisation, before in 1961 being rebranded as Donetsk. Today Donetsk is the capital of the unrecognised 'People's Republic of Donetsk', an illegal, Russian-manufactured territorial entity responsible for many atrocities in Ukraine since the outbreak of war in 2014.

Through the story of John Hughes and the Welsh migrants to Donetsk, I began to dig deeper into the history of Donbas. I discovered the pre-industrial life of the region through the writings of Soviet palaeobotanists, studying their pencil sketches of gigantic tropical plants and swamps to glimpse long-gone vegetal environments that formed the perfect stew to produce coal millions of years later. I studied the maps of industrial geologists, following their delicate swathes of pastel pinks and yellows to learn where the seams of Cretaceous-era limestone, Permian-era gypsum, and (the most sought-after mineral of all) Carboniferous coal shale were distributed across the territory. From the ideologically inflected corpus of Soviet-era industrial historiography, I gleaned insights into the cults of industry that emerged in different parts of this region. I learned about the 'Stakhanovites' who had broken records with their labour, overfulfilling their quotas for mining coal, casting iron, or pouring steel. Drawing on these sources, I constructed a mental map of the region, populated with all the places that I wanted to see and visit: the salt flats of Sloviansk, the coal seams of Lysychansk, the sprawling steelworks of coastal Mariupol.

From 2019, I began to visit the Ukrainian east at least once or twice a year. Led by local historians, geologists, and cave explorers, I discovered the region's overground and subterranean realities, learning first-hand about the places that until then I had only read about in books. In Ivanhrad, I walked the labyrinthine tunnels of the Donetsk region's abandoned gypsum mines. A hundred and eighty metres below the ground in Soledar, I encountered a chilled and sparkling world of hollowed-out salt deposits. The resourceful miners leading our excursion there had developed tourist offerings when the market for salt crashed after 2014. On the front line of the fighting in Toretsk, I joined a tour of Donbas's oldest working coal mine. At the top

of the decrepit headframe (the encased triangular metal structure that sits above a mine), where huge winches had pulled
the half-dressed miners from the depths below, the director
warned us not to go outside, since Russian-backed fighting
groups still fired across the border. All these places, so rich in
history and heritage, now trapped under Russian occupation,
their residents displaced, their industries destroyed.

'What exactly is Donbas?' This is a question that gets posed
again and again in the Soviet-era history textbooks that I've
been using for my research. These works, being Soviet teaching resources, are mostly written in the colonial Russian. In
Russian the question looks like this: Что такое Донбасс?
And sounds like this: *Chto takoe Donbass?* If I had to convey the
intonation of this phrase it would be: What exactly *is* Donbas?
In that 'is' there is the suggestion of doubt, of something that
needs to be cleared up. I've been thinking a lot about this
'What exactly *is*' question, about when and in what contexts it
gets asked. You'd never find it asked about the West Highlands,
for example, or Bavaria; everyone, it's assumed, knows exactly
what those places *are*. Why, then, have historians and writers
been so preoccupied with the existential meaning of this place?
Why were they so keen to answer this question? Why is this
question still being asked so insistently today?

The short answer is colonialism. Donbas, a region that has
historically been located at the intersection of different empires,
has been the focus of multiple colonisation campaigns and
with them, many efforts to re-categorise and rebrand. Donbas,
before it was known as Donbas, was assigned many other politically instrumentalising names. From the sixteenth century it

was known as part of the 'Wild Field', a name that, like the 'Wild West', suggested a place waiting to be 'civilised' through colonisation; for a short time in the eighteenth century the Russian Empire rebranded it as 'Slavianoserbia', a title that referenced the multinational border guards strategically settled in the area; following the forcible incorporation of the Black Sea territories into the empire at the end of the eighteenth century, these lands, in true British colonial style, were reimagined as Novorossiia or 'New Russia'. It was this name, originally intended to attract Slavic settlers to the area, that Putin tried unsuccessfully to revive during his latest phase of Russian settler colonial violence. 'What exactly *is* Donbas' is, then, a question that continues to drive Russia's war of cultural erasure.

Today the term 'Donbas' usually refers to the Donetsk and Luhansk regions in the Ukrainian east. The name is an abbreviation of the geological term 'Donets Coal Basin', first introduced by the French mining engineer Pierre Guillaume Frédéric le Play during expeditions around the region in the 1830s.[2] It wasn't the only name given to these mineral-rich lands at that time. The Ukrainian geologist and colonial administrator Evhraf Kovalevskyi coined 'Donets Mountainous Ridge' in the 1820s to refer to the same territory. 'Donridge' didn't fix itself in the imagination in the same way as 'Donbas', however, and it was the latter that survived into the Soviet period. During the Stalinist 1930s the term 'Donbas' became politically charged, taking on connotations of mechanised hyper-productivity and communist values. Donbas was visualised in propaganda as a beating heart pumping life blood in the form of coal around the communist state's arterial railways. This idea of Donbas as a vital organ, an engine, or a furnace powering the Soviet state became central to the modern imagining of the region and is one that remains relevant to this day.

The annexation of Crimea and the start of Russia's military campaign in the region in 2014 further toxified the term 'Donbas'. With its enthusiastic incorporation by terrorist fighting groups into pro-Russian propaganda, 'Donbas' acquired the taint of military violence and anti-Ukrainian hate. That same year, Olena Stiazhkina, a Donetsk-born historian and writer, rejected the territorial signifier, writing: 'Donbas does not exist. There will be just Ukraine or nothing . . . the word Donbas does not define anything.'[3] With Ukraine's adoption of a package of decommunisation laws in 2015, which aimed to purge the country's public sphere of Soviet place names and monuments, debate around the political correctness of the term intensified. Oleksiy Danilov, the secretary of Ukraine's Council for National Security and Defence, thus condemned the name 'Donbas' in no uncertain terms when speaking in 2021: 'The word "Donbas" is not written in any of our state's regulatory or legal documents,' he declared. 'This is a definition that the Russian Federation has imposed upon us: "the Donbas people", "the choice of Donbas", "Donbas will not be brought to its knees".'[4]

Despite these high-level debates, and despite Russia's full-scale invasion in February 2022, many from the region continue to refer to 'Donbas'. Sitting with friends in a café in western Lviv in summer 2023, I listened to a conversation between a Ukrainian researcher originally from Kharkiv but now based in the United States, and a historian who had, until he was displaced in 2022, lived and worked all his life in the Donetsk region. The US-based researcher expressed her surprise that my friend used 'Donbas' to speak about his native region and admitted that she tried to avoid the term in her own work. My friend explained that he was able to say 'Donbas', since he came from, grew up in, and loved the region, but that outsiders were right to be cautious about what they intended by the word. This conversation reminded me of how terms that were once slurs have been reclaimed by those against whom they have historically been used to do harm. 'Donbas' does carry a lot of baggage, but it also has emancipatory potential. It can be used to Other and objectify, but it can also assert community and a sense of place. In this book, I use it in the knowledge of these contradictions, and never with the intention of causing injury or offence.

There is a Ukrainian version of a popular meme from before the full-scale invasion that shows images of four different kinds of headache. Migraine is shown as a red spot at the front of the head, hypertension is a patch on the crown, stress is a red band around the temples, and 'living next to Russia' is an entire head coloured in red. The joke is serious: Russia has been Ukraine's biggest headache since it gained its independence in 1991. Courting Ukraine's political elites, supporting cross-border business links, and sponsoring cultural and pseudo-cultural organisations promoting Russian language and culture, Russia has done everything in its power to undermine Ukraine's political stability and national unity.[5] Some say that the rhythm of Russia's interference in Ukrainian politics has resulted in a revolution or a war once every dozen or so years – 2004, 2014, 2022. The common factor to all these political milestones? Russia and its refusal to allow Ukraine to disentangle itself from its colonial stranglehold.

With recent dramatic events, some may struggle to remember what happened in 2004. But the Orange Revolution, the mass protests that broke out across Ukraine in response to the corruption, voter intimidation, and electoral fraud that marked the 2004 presidential election run-off vote were in many ways the beginnings of the current war. Disputing the victory of the pro-Russian Party of Regions candidate, Viktor Yanukovych, people across the country took to the streets. The largest protests happened in Kyiv and Lviv, but there were smaller ones in other cities too, including in the east. I remember meeting a group of young Ukrainians who had taken part in the protests at a conference in the Tyrolean mountains in Austria in 2005. They all wore T-shirts emblazoned, in bright orange, with the word 'Tak!', meaning 'Yes!', which had become the symbol of the protests, and radiated positivity and self-confidence. The 2004 demonstrations proved a turning point in Ukraine and a touchstone for protesters during the Maidan Revolution. They were affirmation that self-organisation could realise change in the face of Russian manipulation and domestic corruption.

Ten years later the Russian headache was back with a vengeance. Yanukovych, who had returned to power in 2010, refused to sign the Association Agreement with the European Union in November 2013, ending widespread hopes of closer cooperation with the EU. In response to this perceived act of political treachery, mass protests began on Independence Square in Kyiv, quickly spreading across many cities in Ukraine and becoming a nationwide revolution known as EuroMaidan, or the Revolution of Dignity. Moving more brazenly this time, Russia responded by annexing the Crimean Peninsula and launching a military operation in Donbas. Following years of economic and political investment in the region, the operation found limited traction, and some local fighting groups joined forces with the Russian military.[6] This hybrid military operation, sustained with arms and technologies from Russia, resulted in the occupation of parts of the Donetsk and Luhansk regions and the formation of the pseudo-republics known as the Donetsk and Luhansk 'People's Republics' ('DNR' and 'LNR'). The occupation had catastrophic consequences right across Ukraine. Between 2014 and the escalation of the war in February 2022, more than 14,000 Ukrainian citizens were killed and 43,000 injured, and a further 1.6 million people were displaced from their homes.

Telling the story of Donbas at this moment of time is a political act. The marketplace of information and misinformation about the Ukrainian east stands at the very centre of the ongoing war. Political forces have become even more invested in answering the question, 'What exactly *is* Donbas?' For Putin's Russia, and its war of cultural erasure in the region, Donbas, it disingenuously claims, is an integral part of the 'Russian World'. For the Ukrainian army, fighting fiercely to reclaim this devastated territory, Donbas is unambiguously Ukraine. I am not interested in debating this point: Donbas is, of course, Ukraine. What I am interested in are the many agents and institutions of political and economic exploitation that have contributed towards this present moment: the colonisation of the Wild Field by Russian imperial forces; the region's forcible industrialisation by European capitalists and Soviet managers; the strategic branding of Donbas as a flagship of Soviet industrial modernity; the ruthless impoverishment of local communities by thieving oligarchic elites after communism; and, most importantly for those living in the region today, the political manipulation and coercive violence inflicted by the Russian state since 2014.

This story alone, however, could further contribute to the region's objectification, crystallising it in the eyes of the world as a victim without agency or will. This condition of enforced victimhood is unfortunately not unique. The populations of Palestine, Bosnia, or Northern Ireland share many of the same frustrations about the way they have been reduced to figures of pity and objects of charity, rather than their demands being heard. In this book, I try to think very differently about the places and communities sacrificed to conflict. History emerges on these pages from my encounters and conversations with the many knowledgeable researchers, museum workers, historical enthusiasts, collectors, industry workers, activists, and explorers from the region. I have tried not to erase these individuals in my writing, as often happens to the so-called 'fixers' that journalists and writers employ to provide much-needed local context to their stories. Local knowledge holders are instead centred in this book, unlocking the meaning of this region's special places and past experiences, things only people from and of this place could know.

This book is a product of what I've come to think of as 'care-full' writing. Such writing, for me, means writing for rather than about the people for whom this story matters most, sharing drafts of my work with them, inviting them to edit and correct my texts. Writing in this way involves a kind of vulnerability that academics don't often embrace. It opens you up to criticism from those who know the realities that you're writing about more intimately and profoundly than you do; it makes you face up to the potential of your words, written from places of comfort and privilege, to cause harm. But this approach can also be liberating. In my case, it has allowed me to return to research that, in the immediate aftermath of the full-scale invasion, seemed irrelevant and even unethical. It has allowed me to reconceive my work, not as a parasitic act, exploiting the trauma and suffering of others, but as part of a collaborative venture to bring attention to the complicated history of this rich and beautiful region, a place that has often been reduced to a set of simplistic and misleading stereotypes, a place that has been wrongly dismissed as not worthy of cultural note.

Writing with care has also led me to invite my Ukrainian friends and colleagues to contribute directly to this book. I have asked them to provide their own responses to my writing about their native region, to reflect on what it means to be from and of this place, and what they think of when they think of home. Some authors have responded to this request by writing laconically and academically about their eastern homeland; others have conjured up almost magical-realist portraits of the region. These texts exist as short chapters of their own, punctuating each one of mine; in them I feel that deep attachment to Donbas that I also observed when travelling through this part of Ukraine. I feel my friends' complicated, ambiguous affection for and pride in this place, with its heavy industry that pollutes but also shapes community identity; its landscapes that are damaged but are also familiar, intimate landmarks. As Andrii Prokopov from Mariupol points out in his text, this is a special place, with a special history and special people. I also experienced this region's specialness. It is something I try to render for readers on the pages of this book.

ONE

Mineral Worlds

For me, Donbas is not only a historic region of Ukraine. It is also a unique place where each stone has its own thousand-year history. It is a region whose history is interwoven with the mines and the pits, and which hides a treasure trove of minerals beneath its surface.

The region is famous for its mining heritage, which dates back over three centuries of coal extraction. But Donbas was also one of Eastern Europe's most important centres of ancient mining. The earliest traces of mining here date back to the Stone Age, and are linked to the extraction and manufacturing of flint. In the Bronze Age, a group of ancient mines and a mining and metallurgy complex were founded on the copper ores of the Bakhmut Basin. During the Iron Age and the early Middle Ages, this area became a centre for the extraction and smelting of iron ores. From the end of the sixteenth to the beginning of the seventeenth century, the Tor and later the Bakhmut salt trade began to develop.

In 1664, the first state-owned salt factory was built on the Tor salt lakes. At the end of the nineteenth century, large deposits of rock salt were discovered, prompting the rapid construction of salt mines in the area. From the end of the eighteenth century, systematic geological studies of the Donetsk Ridge began, and from the middle of the nineteenth century, large-scale industrial development took place. A huge industrial region grew up on the foundations of the Donets Coal Basin. This was the origin story of many of the region's smaller mining towns as well as its gigantic metallurgical complexes.

My journeys through the depths of Donbas started more than ten years ago when I decided to share my impressions and knowledge of this incredible region. In my blog 'Mines and Pits of

Donbas' I research and write about the secrets of this industrial region of Ukraine. In articles, photos, and specialist publications, I try to demonstrate the beauty and value of every corner of Donbas. This is not just a story of mines and quarries, but a journey into a world where traditions meet modernity, where work meets rest. Today, sadly, Donbas has become a huge wound on the territory of our country and a tragedy of divided destinies.

Mykhailo Kulishov

Horlivka, Donetsk region (occupied since 2014)

NEAR LYSYCHANSK in the Luhansk region, there is a place called 'Fox Beam' (Lysiacha Balka), also known as 'the cradle of Donbas'. Fox Beam, named for the many foxes who roamed this land, is the mythologised birthplace of Donbas's coal industry and the location of the region's first coal mine, sunk here in 1792. On a cloudless summer's day in July 2021, I am walking along the Beam as part of a group led by Mykola Skuridin, a sprightly local historian dressed in England football top, shorts, and plastic flip-flops. Mykola is helping us pick our way through the undergrowth to a place where you can still surface-mine coal. He speaks constantly as we walk, taking the ascent in his stride, while I scramble, breathless, up the bank. A fount of knowledge about Lysychansk's mining history, he is in his element talking to interested foreigners like me about this special place that most of us would otherwise never get to see. His blue eyes sparkle against his tanned, smiling face. He gestures for us to move on, promising that we are almost there, clearly excited at the surprise that awaits us.

The Luhansk region, part of the Eurasian steppe belt, is thick with heat in July and most of our group are dressed more for the beach than a cross-country hike. Mykola's football strip shines like a beacon ahead, however, and helps us find our way through the fir, fern, and elder that has formed a tangled carpet on the forest floor. As we walk, we criss-cross a rust-coloured stream – its iron ores have stained the clay bed beneath an iridescent, unworldly orange. Finally, we arrive at a brittle white rock face; seams of black coal snake across its higher reaches. Here, Mykola produces a coal pick – an object from the local museum, he tells us – and skips gazelle-like up the rock to hack coal from the cliff, stashing the chunks in a plastic bag. Offering his haul around the group, he explains that this is some of the best-quality anthracite to be found in Europe. My lump of coal, gradually disintegrating into a powdery mass, sits beside me now in Scotland as I write.

Donbas has long been associated with coal. The much lusted-after fossil fuel resonates across the region's toponymical landscape. The rock has given its name to cities and villages in the eastern territory, including Vuhledar, from the Ukrainian for coal (*vuhillia*), Shakhtarsk, from the Ukrainian for miner (*shakhtar*) and Antratsyt, from the Ukrainian for anthracite (*antratsyt*).[1] Even the name Donbas itself, a shortening of Donets Coal Basin (*Donets'kyi vuhil'nyi basein*), references the mighty mineral. Coal formed part of the cultural imagination of Donbas from the nineteenth century onward. After the revolution, propaganda art fetishised the region as an inexhaustible

source of the valuable fossil fuel. From the Stalin period, people were subjected to an onslaught of documentary film and literature celebrating the feats of the region's superhuman miners, square-jawed Stakhanovs and Izotovs overfulfilling their quotas by forty times. Donbas came to mean coal, and coal to mean Donbas. The two were industrially forged together.

The emergence of coal as the dominant association of Donbas is, however, the result of extractivist storytelling, a reductive kind of meaning-making that imagines places only in terms of their most commodifiable component parts. If we delve beneath the surface of this region, we find mineral worlds that did not capture the colonial imagination in the same way as coal but are nevertheless fundamental parts of Donbas's long geological development. These sedimentary layers form chapters from the distant past. They describe land-scapes from 'deep time' – sometimes desiccated and lifeless, sometimes lush and tropical – that left traces of their multi-species' lives beneath the ground. To explore these beneaths is to encounter the many identities of a place now exclusively associated with industrial extraction, depletion, and war. It is the recovery of a rich and long history of environmental trans-formation, intermittent erasure, and periodic geological and ecological reconstitution.

◈

People often think that 'Donbas' was a Soviet invention. But the term, and the associated idea of the region as a site of mineral extraction and profit-making, in fact dates back much earlier. One of the most important figures in Donbas's trans-formation into an industrial commodity was the Ukrainian geologist Evhraf Kovalevskyi.[2] Born in a village near Kharkiv in 1790, Kovalevskyi completed his studies at the empire's most prestigious school of mineral extraction research, the Gorny (Mining) Institute in St Petersburg. This elite-forming institu-tion produced the geologists responsible for sourcing minerals to power the industrial engine of the Russian Empire. The political significance of this work was reflected in the fact that many of its graduates transitioned into politics, using their knowledge to direct economic policy in the rapidly industri-alising imperial state. This remained the case even into the twenty-first century. Two hundred years after Kovalevskyi, Vladimir Putin, the author of Russia's war against Ukraine, would also graduate from this same school of mining expertise.

In 1816, Kovalevskyi began work at the imperial headquarters of mineral extraction, the Department of Mining and Salt Affairs. This bureaucratic-sounding unit was one of the most powerful departments in the quickly industrialising Russian Empire, responsible for mineral excavation across the vast territory of the colonies, from the iron and copper ore quarries in Siberia to the coal mines of central Kazakhstan. From this crucible of colonial administration, Kovalevskyi would return, two years later, to his native Ukrainian east, tasked with identifying the location of the iron ore and coal deposits that could feed Luhansk's emerging steelmaking enterprises. Kovalevskyi undertook this prospecting work simultaneously with academic research into the mineral composition of the region's subsoils. During their expeditions around the region, his team of geologists sunk boreholes deep into the earth, testing the composition of the samples they drew. Based on this research, Kovalevskyi produced one of the first stratigraphical surveys of the Donets Mountain Ridge, a map which revealed for the first time the region's mineral-rich sedimentary foundations.[3]

Kovalevskyi's 'Petrographic Map of the Donets Mountain Ridge' marks the transformation of the Donbas region from an object of 'scientific interest' into an extraction resource, a commodity for colonial exploitation (see plate section for reproduction).[4] It was not the only region to be commodified in this way. Resource-rich regions all over Western Europe, from the oil-shale lands of West Lothian in Scotland to the coal deposits of Upper Silesia, were undergoing similar conceptual transformations at that time. But more than any other map of the territory that preceded or postdated it, this stratigraphic portrait paved the way for the industrial exploitation of Donbas, with a proliferation in the years that followed of mining infrastructures and an influx of labourers from all over the Russian Empire and further abroad. Charmingly picturesque in its muted colours and delicate calligraphy, this map was, then, a harbinger of mechanised industrial change. Following its publication in the early nineteenth century, capitalist industrialists would pour into Donbas, turning the region inside out in their attempts to excavate their fortunes from the mineral-rich ground beneath.

In the summer of 2021, as Russian troops began to gather menacingly around the edges of Ukraine, I journeyed around the region depicted in Kovalevskyi's map with Mykhailo (Misha) Kulishov, a researcher and cave explorer. Misha's interest in Donbas's mineral history had emerged during his teenage years in his native city of Horlivka, a coal-mining settlement, which since 2014 had been occupied by Russian military and fighting groups. As we drove along, swerving and occasionally hitting potholes that made our bones jolt, Misha told me about the expeditions he had taken around Horlivka's abandoned mines as a young man. His troop of intrepid explorers would descend into the Earth's depths, lugging a canoe to allow them to pass parts of the mines that had flooded since their closure. It was in these recesses that Misha fell in love with the region's geological history, a history he would bring alive for me with his encyclopaedic knowledge as we travelled across the territory.

The swathes of pink, yellow, and green on Kovalevskyi's map speak of the geological realities that formed in this region over millions of years. The wide belt of pink that follows the undulations of the Siverskyi Donets – a river that stretches from near Belgorod in Russia, merging with the fast-flowing Don before emptying in the shallows of the Azov Sea – indicates Cretaceous-era chalk and limestone that lie beneath the ground. In the ungraspable vastness of geological time, the Cretaceous period, taking place between a mere 145.5 and 65.5 million years ago, is a relatively recent planetary experience. The mineral deposits that it has gifted the Earth thus lie relatively near to the surface. When humans first started quarrying these materials, there was no need for boreholes and mines. It was enough to scratch the topsoil to reveal the startling white and dusky pinks of the brittle rocks beneath the ground.

Bilokuzmynivka, located in the map's top right-hand corner between today's occupied Bakhmut and front-line Sloviansk, is a rocky outcrop where the earth's chalk deposits dramatically break through the crust. An aberration in a series of modest chalk hills that line the right bank of the pine-bordered Bilenka River, Bilokuzmynivka is a truly awesome sight. As we arrive by car from the west, the jagged, dirty white peaks rise from the ground like a blast of choral song. It is easy to understand how this chalk mountain has lodged itself in human imagination and drawn peace-seekers to it over the centuries, hermits and other kinds of recluses. But, as Misha explains, the real fascination of Bilokuzmynivka is in its mineral detail, something that cannot be appreciated from a distance, and must be contemplated up close. We leave the car, meeting a blast of steppe heat, and begin to climb.

Ninety million years ago when the deposits that would eventually form Belokuzmynivka were accumulating, Ukraine was mostly covered by sea. This sea was a warm and life-welcoming place cut through by sunlight much more intense than that which bears down on us now, searing the skin on the back of my neck on this summer's day. This Cretaceous sea abounded with life: it was filled with rays, sharks, and ray-finned fish called teleosts, as well as marine reptiles like ichthysosaurs and plesiosaurs. It was also replete with less dynamic life: sea urchins, starfish, and crustaceans of many variations thrived. Most abundant of all, however, were the microscopic single-celled organisms encased in tiny shells made of calcite (calcium carbonate). Across millions of years, as the waves of this sunlit sea swelled and crashed, these plankton died in their droves, their lime skeletons coming to form a thick layer on the sea floor. As this calcium-rich sediment built up, it rose closer to the surface, slowly baking into rock.[5]

It is mind-bending to think that, having scrambled the final steep incline to reach the top of Bilokuzmynivka, we are standing, sweaty but exhilarated, on what would have once been the shell-lined bottom of the Cretaceous sea. Misha casts around to find me a fossil to take home as a souvenir: marine fauna, such as ammonites, belemnites, and sea urchins have left their impressions everywhere on the soft white rock, postcards from another geological time. While humans have tended to show deference to this geological monument, they have not treated flint, its mineral fellow traveller, which forms lines of morse code along the rock face, with the same respect. Misha tells me that in the 1960s, Soviet archaeologists uncovered Bronze Age workshops near to Bilokuzmynivka containing remnants of flint excavated from this site. I draw my hand across the jagged, protruding stone, and find it surprisingly cool by contrast with the warm, baked chalk in which it resides.

Chalk was of course not treated so reverently everywhere. The discovery of its uses for whitewashing houses, making putty, and manufacturing paint, as well as in the production of cement, made it a desirable commodity even from ancient times.[6] Under Soviet rule, chalk deposits were quarried for phosphorites that could be used in mineral fertiliser. Phosphorites, Misha explains, like potassium salts, are sometimes referred to as 'fertility stones', seemingly inexhaustible sources of mineral nourishment for fields. At the Chalk Flora nature reserve, located along the gently billowing Milk Ravine, named after the white chalk deposits that patch the landscape here, chalk bricks have been cut by hand from the deposit. These same hands have engraved the chalk with cryptic messages, numbers and initials whose meaning has been lost over time. In the baking steppe heat, the exploitative and exhausting labour practices that transformed this mineral-rich site resound in the landscape.

At the quarry, we meet Serhii Lymanskyi, Chalk Flora's dedicated director and a keen photographer. Serhii is dressed in military fatigues emblazoned with the reserve's emblem: his arm patch features one of the park's iconic chalk pines, a beaver, and a golden eagle. This army apparel at first strikes me as incongruous. Serhii's job seems far from militaristic. His descriptions of patrolling the park's territory early in the morning, when the mists still lie thick on the chalky ground, on the contrary, seem headily romantic. But, as he explains, his work often entails confrontation. He talks about his ongoing battles with groups who threaten the park with careless camp-fires and illegal hunting trips, how he and his family have been physically intimated by these individuals, who are often polit-ically connected, and how he's sometimes not slept for several nights through worry. Protecting this endangered landscape from those who would exploit it for their own pleasure and privilege does indeed seem like a military operation – one that requires considerable courage and competence.

Recognised by governmental decree in 1988, Chalk Flora was, before the full-scale invasion, one of the only places in Ukraine where vegetation growing from soils formed of Cretaceous rock could still be found in a satisfactory condition. Among the 490 kinds of plant life growing in the reserve are several endangered plants such as oak-leaf tulips, yellow-flow-ering Don gorse, and purple, pendant-headed fritillaria.[7] Among this vegetation, however, one also finds deposits of a very different sort. As we wander through the park, Serhii points out places where shattered tank windows and projectiles lie abandoned on the ground. The Ukrainian army occupied the strategic height in 2014 as it fought with advancing Russian-backed forces in the east. Rather than clear these vestiges of war away, Serhii has left them in place: 'I hope that they will act as a warning of sorts, reminding visitors to the park how awful war is and how it should be avoided at all costs.'

The talismanic power of these objects was sadly not strong enough. In spring 2022 the park was once more engulfed by violence as Russia escalated its war against Ukraine. In April, Misha messaged me to say that a bomb had hit Serhii's wooden house while he was out on his dawn patrols, erasing a life's archive of belongings, including the camera with which he'd photograph the steppe, and killing his beloved budgerigar

Zhorochko. Serhii was forced to leave for a safer region of Ukraine, from where he began to fundraise for parks that, like his, were caught in the crossfire of military conflict. More detritus of war is building up in Chalk Flora. Grenades, projectiles, and mortars are accumulating amid the steppe gorse and horsetails. Unlike the Cretaceous-era deposits, which speak of the quiet environmental evolutions of millennia past, this Russian-inflicted sedimentary layer tells a categorically violent story. It will be up to future generations to excavate the history of this multispecies catastrophe, and to hold the guilty accountable for the environmental devastation.

My first geological expedition with Misha was to an abandoned gypsum mine at the south-west edge of Kovalevskyi's lemon-coloured Permian system. The Ivanhrad gypsum mine (just south of Bakhmut) can be entered via several 'adits', horizontal entrances that also served as drainage, ventilation and extraction systems while the mine was functioning. As we approach one of these low-ceilinged openings, Misha explains that this mine was owned in pre-revolutionary times by one of the large alabaster-production companies belonging to the East Prussian engineer Edmund Farke. It was further developed once the Soviets came to power. In the 1930s, a narrow-gauge railway was built to transport gypsum to the Artemivsk-1 station; this was replaced in the 1940s to early 1950s by a steam locomotive that travelled along the same tracks. When the mine stopped operating in the 1960s, the railway was dismantled. As we enter the mine's cool antechamber, I realise, to my surprise, that we are moving forwards in time: the tunnels closest to the entranceway are the oldest, dating back to the nineteenth century, while the most recently mined sections, excavated in the 1960s, are hidden away in the underground system's furthest recesses.

The Permian-era gypsum that the colonial owners of these mines so desired was formed between 299 million and 250 million years ago. The life-giving sea that would wash over the region during the Cretaceous period, leaving its chalk deposits in the ground, had retreated from the mountainous Donetsk country to what are today the territories of the Caucasus and Central Russia. Only a narrow gulf stretched like a long tongue across the territory, ending its journey in nowadays Bakhmut. The climate at that time was hot and arid and this gulf periodically lost its connection with the sea and dried out completely. All that would be left of the water source was a string of lagunas and lakes. Deposits of salt settled and crystallised at their desiccated base. Where the soil's mineral elements differed slightly, gypsum occurred, forming thick beds and clumps of crystals.[8]

In the mine, signs of human interference are everywhere. Metre-long scars mark the walls: these are the exposed remains of drill holes into which dynamite would have been placed to blast apart the rock. Explosions took place at night, while few workers were present, and the shattered gypsum was collected and loaded into railway carts the next day. As we walk deeper into the Soviet section of the mine, we see hooks from insulators and electrical-wiring fasteners bleeding rust down the alabaster walls. Occasionally I step over part of an old railway sleeper on which the rock would have been transported in trolleys out of the mine. Historic human interference continues to resonate in this underground world. The tunnels

have several sinkholes caused by the activity of groundwater and precipitation. Where the roofs of the hollowed-out passageways have fallen in, sculptural 'gravitational cones', which look like mini-pyramids of rubble, have been created. We stop to photograph one in which swallows have made their nests. The way the light falls on it from above makes it look like an art installation.

Meditating on this gravitational cone, I am aware of the intersecting geological, political, and social processes that have led to this precise moment. The incremental expansion of cartographical knowledge, including the development of geological mapping, created the conditions for the region's subsoil to be visualised and excavated by generations of colonial labourers, toiling beneath the ground in these man-made caves. For around a century, workers detonated explosives and hauled gypsum out of this mine, gradually extending the labyrinth of tunnels beneath the land's surface. It seems the integrity of the mines was actually greater when they were functioning; miners made sure that the water that could cause ceilings to fall in was pumped out and that the walls were properly propped. With the abandonment of the mines in the 1960s, nature was left to redefine these spaces. Sinkholes opened up through which tumbleweed fell in summer, and water flooded their lower reaches, creating underwater pools across which the light of our torches now dances.

While some gypsum mines were abandoned to their fates – frequented only by bats, foxes, and the occasional curious geologist – others were adapted in the twentieth century for new kinds of mechanised production. At the end of the 1940s, the abandoned gypsum mines under Bakhmut were given new purpose in the emerging economy of socialist consumerism. Undeterred by the flooding in many of the mine's cavities, the Soviet Council of Ministers decided to turn these man-made caves into the USSR's first manufacturing plant and storage facility for 'Soviet Champagne'. This sweet sparkling wine, produced using Crimean and other southern Ukrainian vines, became an iconic element of the Soviet-era festive table, an essential purchase for any birthday, festival, and, of course, New Year. Over the next twenty years, Artemivsk (Bakhmut) Champagne Wine Factory gradually increased its production to 10 million bottles a year. By the early 1970s it was exporting its elite produce, entirely manufactured in the excavated underground gypsum caves, not only to communist eastern Europe, but also to the capitalist world, in particular Belgium, Switzerland, and Austria.[9]

The entangled industrial history of the gypsum mines in Bakhmut make visiting the site a palimpsestic experience. Like a magic-eye puzzle, you can adjust your view to see the history of German alabaster production out of one eye and the history of Soviet winemaking out of the other. The chiselled gypsum walls, along with elements of the historic mining infrastructure, are painted lurid colours and decorated with folksy murals featuring scenes of drunken revelry. One particularly thick pillar of gypsum is carved into the face of Bacchus, the god's hooded eyes steadily observing the fermentation process. In another atmospherically lit chamber, a heavy wooden table is surrounded by high-backed chairs, apparently used for high-profile dégustations. The uplighting in the room draws attention to the historic drill holes in the walls. Different strands from the mine's industrial past intertwine here in a way that is both uncanny and poetic: extraction, production, and performative consumption are concentrated into one single space and time.

When Russia launched its full-scale assault against Bakhmut in 2023, systematically razing the city to the ground in its desperate attempt at a strategic victory, I found myself thinking again of these gypsum mines. The Permian deposits, extracted for their plaster-making properties in the nineteenth century and adapted as wine cellars in the twentieth, were being reinvented once more, this time as bomb shelters and dormitories for those who had lost their homes. Videos surfaced of people gathered in the caves, eating, sleeping, and talking quietly together. Later, more troubling scenes circulated online, of Russian mercenaries pillaging the factory's wine stores. The walls of the caves, marked with scars of historic explosions, shuddered again with another kind of colonial violence.

If gypsum had come to define Bakhmut by the late nineteenth century, salt was the city's most historic industry. The naturally occurring salt around Tor (today's Sloviansk) attracted settlers to the region from at least as far back as the thirteenth century. From the 1700s, when the Tor and Bakhmut settlements were created to defend the empire's southern border, salt was produced through solar evaporation methods, and later by rock-salt mining, for trade with visiting merchants.[10] Writing in 1869, Ivan Levakovskii, a soil scientist at Kharkiv University, dedicated one of his extensive essays on 'southern Russia' (today's Ukraine) to the region's salt lakes. 'This part of the Torets Valley is covered with salt lakes and springs,' he wrote in his field note. 'All of the soil here is saturated with salt particles, so saltwater oozes into even the shallowest pits. In spring, there are up to ten lakes here, of which six, with the onset of summer heat, dry up, leaving swamps covered with salt silt and mud.'[11]

Misha is keen that I see one of these desiccated salt swamps, so we are in the car again, driving south to the village of Oleksandro-Kalynove, just outside Kostiantynivka and around fifty kilometres from the front line. It seems salt was boiled from local lakes here from the 1880s by the local landowner, who built a small factory (now long gone) on the land. Today the salt's unmediated presence in the ground creates an uncanny effect: it looks as though a makeshift ice rink has been laid in the middle of the sun-scorched steppe. The salt is as coarse to the touch as sandpaper and has cracked in the summer heat. At the edges of the marsh, *solonets'* – or as I know it, marsh samphire – stretches up its knobbly red-and-green stalks, making beautiful shadow play against the white beneath.

The Russian name for *solonets'* is *soleros*, translating roughly as 'grown where there is salt'. This name reveals the historic function of the plant in this part of the world, for while it was used in glass and soap-making in the UK, eaten with olive oil and fish in the Netherlands and France, in Ukraine it was an organic signpost to the salty springs that would inevitably be located nearby.[12] These springs were a historic source of mineral extraction: traditionally, a well would be sunk from which salt brine could be taken for evaporation in shallow, artificial pools. In Oleksandro-Kalynove, an enterprising local resident, Andrii Taraman, has reconstructed one of these wells for visiting tourists. Before the war turned this village into a battlefield, groups of schoolchildren could follow signposts to this spot, lower a bucket down the wooden shaft, emulating the historic processes for sourcing salt, and haul out salty brine to evaporate under the scorching steppe sun.

It is not just humans making lives for themselves amid the region's salt deposits. A short distance away, the banks of Sloviansk's salt lakes, which intermingle here with the flood-plains of the Kolontaivka River, are populated by colonies of water birds. Profiting from the thickets of reeds and cattails that thrive in the salty pools, terns and waders arrive here in their thousands each year to make their homes. To the excitement of local ornithologists, the wetlands have also attracted the black-winged stilt, a species of bird endangered throughout Ukraine. This long-beaked, spindly legged specimen is depicted next to a sprig of samphire in a cheerful mural on the main road through the city. Like so many other creatures, these birds are now facing displacement because of Russia's war. Incessant bombing, which has brought ruination to Sloviansk for the second time in just ten years, has also degraded the land in this area, bringing defoliants and chemical contaminants that have toxified the waters and compromised the sandpipers' and other birds' natural habitats.

Artemsil' in Soledar – a city that takes its name from the Ukrainian word for salt, *sil'* – is one of Ukraine's oldest working salt mines. Dating back to the pre-revolutionary period, when the smaller French-managed Briantsev pit was in operation here, it has been emptying the earth of its supposedly inexhaustible white mineral for over 140 years. After 2014, when exports of salt to Russia ceased following the outbreak of war, the mine, which, along with others in Soledar, produced around 80 per cent of Ukraine's salt, faced growing financial precarity. To substitute its rapidly decreasing sales, it opened its doors to visiting tourist excursions. Misha has signed us up to one of these tours, along with a group of excitable tourists from Kharkiv. After donning hard hats and, for those who wish to, blue housecoats emblazoned with the mine's emblem, we descend 180 metres below the ground and emerge into a chilled (16°C) and sparkling world of hollowed-out salt deposits.

The route of our tourist excursion is a curious subterranean spectacle. A series of tunnels created by industrial diggers connects several chambers featuring tourist attractions that the miners themselves have curated. In one of the central tunnels, a local folk artist has installed a salt carving of Shubin, the gnome-like mythological spirit of the mines about whom folk tales have been written since the nineteenth century. Another alcove hosts a huge cube of transparent salt that the miners discovered while they were digging. One of the most surprising installations is a salt chapel – 'a fake for the tourists', Misha whispers in my ear – that has been carved into the rock, replete with chandelier, altar, and icons. Our guide tells us that somewhere else in these labyrinthine depths are hotel rooms where guests can stay overnight to treat respiratory and other chronic health problems. 'Scientific studies have proven that breathing the salt improves longevity,' he explains. After standing exposed in the hot Soledar sun all morning, I begin to fantasise about lying down in this salty cave.

As the tourists clamour to have their photographs taken next to the folk art, Misha calls me to one side to examine the salt walls. The rotating drills have created beautiful effects in these tunnels, marking the white-grey chambers with regular undulating lines that remind me of the approaching tide of

the sea. Elsewhere, the natural salts in the rock have reacted with water in the air, causing them to dissolve and evaporate, forming fluffy crystals on the surface of the walls. This efflorescence forms textured streaks that reach to join hands other across the man-made shaft: Misha tells me miners call the streaks 'salt tears', a name that seems particularly poignant given the difficult fate the mines are facing today.

The tour concludes in a cavernous sixty-foot-high room in which the miners have installed an exhibition of objects related to the historic salt industry. The carved-out vitrines in the salt walls hold pages from the mine's past: cloth caps and shoes made from woven tree bark worn by the mine's first labourers; collars and bits suffered by pit ponies; and unique mineral finds discovered during mining, such as a section of salt cut through with sculptural lignite coal, a fossil that Misha tells me should really be housed in a geological museum.

The most compelling object in the room, however, is a monumental salt slab into which steps have been carved to create a podium. It was from this mineral stage that Soviet politicians addressed a delegation of industrial managers in 1925, commanding them to dig ever deeper into the resource-rich depths of the country in their drive to manifest the dreamed-of bright future that was communism. The delegation's clapping, I imagine, would have echoed around this vast chamber, given the extraordinary acoustics. Generation upon generation of political opportunists have appropriated these mineral depths in their efforts to dictate the political meaning of this region. As recently as January 2023, Russia's mercenary Wagner group temporarily took control of the mine, photographing themselves here in staged poses. Since the region's occupation, the mines have sustained serious damage; it is not clear yet what is left of their historic infrastructure. In the tunnels the salt tears creep their efflorescent paths down the walls, a mineral timeline of this slow and devastating war.

Chalk, limestone, gypsum, and salt . . . it is not for nothing that Donbas has been called a treasure trove of mineral riches. Yet it is coal that has endured in the political and cultural imagination of the place. Kovalevskyi's petrographic map helps to understand the reasons why. The green swathes that comprise a large part of this map mark the Carboniferous formations in which clay shale and coal are located. This part of Donbas was found to contain three kinds of coal: coking, lean, and anthracite of a quality rarely encountered in Europe.[13] The cartographic documentation of coal's presence in the land in the 1820s formed an effective invitation to industrialist capitalists to descend on the region in the decades that followed, seeking to excavate their fortunes from the region's mineral depths. Today the territory is cross-hatched by an expansive network of coal mines and pits. Their iconic headframes and slag heaps form irregular verticals on the otherwise flat steppe landscape.

As the environmental critic Darya Tsymbalyuk has remarked, coal is a 'more-than-human' environmental archive.[14] It contains within itself the traces of the abundant plant and animal life that thrived in the near-tropical conditions of the Carboniferous era. Having grown up near the coal-rich South Wales Valleys, I find it strange that I never questioned what coal was as a child. It always seemed to me a material inevitability, a banal natural product in the landscape that was awaiting extraction to be activated into something useful. But Tsymbalyuk is right that it is much more than that. Coal is a portal into another world of animal and plant life no longer with us, into otherworldly times. The black rock that Mykola surface-mined in Lysychansk is thus a memento mori from deep time. Its brittle layers, disintegrating into sparkling powder, speak of many lives, many passings.

Coal formed in a period even earlier than chalk and salt. The Carboniferous era is usually dated from the end of the Devonian period, 358.9 million years ago, to the beginning of the Permian period, 60 million years later. In what would become the Ukrainian east, this was a time of great flourishing. The Devonian sea, covering most of Eurasia, whose deep bottom teemed with all kinds of now extinct crustacean life, was gradually lowering to expose small islands of dry land. Along today's Donbas there was a sea bank dense with bogs. These spongy wetlands, comprising partially decayed organic matter from the sea's base, were extraordinary sources of new life. Over time all kinds of plants took root here, from explosive ferns to the creeping mosses familiar to us today. The tropical climate – an endless summer of close humidity and constant rain – provided ideal conditions for prehistoric trees. These now extinct giants – scaly-trunked *Lepidodendrons* and *Sigillaria*, like huge, tufted potato spores – covered the region, forming thick, monotonous forests.[15]

It was the layering and layering of these strange trees, mosses, and ferns, which – having lived their lives and accumulated the sun's energy like batteries – died and sank to the bottom of the Carboniferous bog that would eventually form the region's coal. As the bogs drained away, the carbonised, peat-like remains of these plants were compressed by yet more falling trees, building pressure and heat that would bake the coal like an oven. Periodically, over the millennia, the sea would once more sweep the region's surface, shifting these deposits to deep underwater, before lowering again and beginning the process of bog formation and forest growth anew. Repeated around 200 times, this process created layers of coal all over the region. These are the same layers that would be documented by Kovalevskyi and fellow geologists millennia later, beginning the era of intense industrial extraction.

The lure of coal has brought various colonial agents to Donbas, many of whom have laid claim to the discovery of the region's 'black gold'. There are multiple iterations of the historical narrative, all of which invariably foreground intrepid male protagonists.[16] The most widely disseminated story in Soviet times was that of the Russian geologist Grigorii Kapustin, who was said to have presented the mineral to the Russian Emperor Peter I (also known as 'the Great') during the Azov campaigns (1695–6). The 'worldly' tsar, the story has it, was able to identify the rock as coal and utter the fateful (though undocumented) words: 'This material, if not for us, then for our descendants will have utility.'[17] There is still a gold-plated monument to Kapustin, cradling the 'useful mineral' in his hands, in the coal-mining settlement of Lysychansk. This monument, one suspects, will be quickly dispensed with if and when the Ukrainian army recaptures the city, as part of the official state policy of de-russifying – and so decolonising – the country's cultural memory.

The myth itself has already been debunked. Misha and fellow historian from Lysychansk, Mykola Lomako, revealed in a local history journal a few years ago that coal was in fact first discovered by Ukrainian salt merchants near Bakhmut in the 1720s. What's more, there was indigenous knowledge of coal in the landscape, which dated back much further than this. As they write: 'local residents may not only have known about the earthen coal seams present in numerous detachments of mountain rocks but may very likely have mined them as well.'[18] Working with historical maps, Misha and Mykola have pinpointed the present-day location of coal's discovery in Skelevata Beam in Toretsk. In July 2021 Misha and I travel to Toretsk to visit the site where a memorial plaque has been installed and for a tour of the Central Mine, the oldest working coal mine in the Donbas region.

As we approach Toretsk, the roadblocks manned by Ukrainian army officers become more frequent and checks more rigorous. Toretsk is located just ten kilometres from the military border and the presence of the conflict is immediately more tangible. On arrival we are greeted by the director of the mine. Contrary to my expectations, he is not a jaded local bureaucrat but an enthusiastic, generous guide who is clearly delighted and proud to have a foreign guest to show around. In our party there are two other lively local tourists: Svitlana, who teaches philosophy at the local mining academy and is Toretsk's foremost local historian, and her excited seven-year-old grandson, Nestor. As we tour the mine's territory, I realise that despite growing up in a place where mines were active until the 1980s, I have never actually been in the vicinity of working mining machinery. The oceanic roar of the coal descending the metal slide and filling the back of a truck and the glittering coal flecks that float down from the sky are all things I've only seen in documentary films in heritage centres. When a miner appears from a doorway in just a pair of shorts – the heat inside the mine is 42°C – for a second it feels like a poorly conceived museum reconstruction.

The mine is, however, a historic relic. The director accompanies us to the top of an enclosed headframe, where we can see impossibly huge winding drums turning as they raise the conveyances from the mine shaft below. Misha suggests that we go up onto the roof to take in the view, but the director forbids it: sometimes Russian-armed fighting groups shoot across the border. Instead, he invites us to enter a vestibule where a woman in her thirties sits in front of a remarkable array of Soviet-era gauges, buttons, and switches. The machinery looks worryingly vintage, given the fact that hundreds of men are currently working 200 metres beneath the ground. I notice that one of the frames on the dashboard is occupied by a fading icon of the Virgin Mary and Baby Jesus – a traditional decoration for this kind of high-risk place of work, even in the Soviet era. I hope that they are paying attention today and safeguarding the wellbeing of those working in this ageing institution.

The director explains that plans were once afoot to close the mine and replace it with some safer form of employment. As soon as the war broke out in 2014, however, with the front line of the fighting just a few kilometres away and outbursts of violence on that border still commonplace, investors, both public and private, were no longer prepared to risk sinking their money into the town. As we say our goodbyes, the director encourages me to visit again next time I'm in Ukraine: 'Maybe we'll have a macaroni factory here by then,' he jokes. As we drive off, I find myself thinking of Nestor, and ask Misha if there is any other form of employment in the town. No, he answers, this is a monotown, the mine is currently the only source of jobs. With so few options, symbolic gestures such as the installation of the plaque have had enormous social significance. As we get out of the car to look at the memorial, Svitlana tells me about her plans to have the site recognised as a preservation zone. She beams and explains how happy it makes her to know she lives in a historic town.

Asia Bazdyrieva, a Ukrainian art historian and ecological critic, has written about the 'resourcification' of Ukraine. By resourcification, Bazdyrieva means not only the processes of mineral extraction that turned the country into a tradeable resource, but also the crystallisation of Ukraine in the world's imagination as a commodity for exchange with no political will or agency of its own.[19] This idea applies particularly well to Donbas. The resource-rich region has often been imagined in terms of its extraction potential: the profits and power to be accumulated through the mining and quarrying of its gypsums, salts, chalks, and coals. The historical roots of this process can be found in the stratigraphic mapping and resource surveying of Kovalevskyi and other colonial state actors. But it also continues to resonate today. The Russian war that is now raging in the east can be seen as an extension of this same thinking, centred around resourcification. Russia attributes little agency to the communities of Donbas to decide their own fate: it rather sees the region as an asset to be acquired and appropriated, to be traded in exchange for political influence.

In the picturesque village of Kryva Luka, from where Misha and his colleague Yana run their ecotourism firm, a radically different understanding of the region is possible. Nestled in the hills between Sloviansk and Bakhmut, Kryva Luka overlooks a flat, forested steppe that is decidedly un-industrial, worlds away from the mechanical inferno of Dziga Vertov's documentary *Enthusiasm: A Donbas Symphony* (1931), or Valentyn Vasyanovych's post-apocalyptic feature film *Atlantis* (2019), both of which have envisioned Donbas for global audiences. As we lunch on potato and mushroom pyrogi that a neighbour has delivered in a basket covered with a chequered napkin, Misha asks me what foreigners think of when they hear the word 'Donbas'. I hesitate. I want to say something that will make him happy, but the truth is, of course, heavy industry and war. Misha and Yana were working to shift these associations before the full-scale invasion, introducing foreign visitors like me to the geological and historical riches of this region. Now the association with war has crystallised. Excavating other stories that reside in the mineral-rich landscape has become more difficult than ever.

Before we leave Kryva Luka, Misha takes me to see the collection of rocks and minerals that he has collected for Yana during their years working together. This remarkable display, which contains sculptural chunks of transparent salt, rolled fingers of chalk and even a Soviet-era glass jar in which crystals of gypsum and salt have formed, is housed in a glass-fronted cupboard inside the village's cheerful community centre. As Misha explains, this is his second collection of geological treasures from Donbas. He was forced to abandon the first in Horlivka when the city was occupied in 2014: it had simply not been possible to include it among the essential items that he and his family took with them when they were displaced.

In February 2022, Misha was displaced for a second time, this time from Bakhmut where he had rebuilt his life and run together with Yana a successful business. I don't know what happened to his collection of rocks and minerals: it feels too difficult a question to ask.

TWO

Colonial Entanglements

We don't get to choose where we are born. It just so happens that I was born in the Ukrainian east. In Donbas.

As a child growing up, you see the headframes and the slag heaps. You smell the coking ovens, hear the hum of the blast furnaces and the clanking of the train wheels. And all this against a backdrop of endless fields that blend in with the steppe. When you're small you think the whole world looks like this. It's only when you grow up that you realise this isn't the case. And when you're older yet, you realise that this is a special place.

This is a place with special people, with a special character, with a special outlook on life, with a special culture. It's a place with a special history that is complicated and multinational. Your mother sings to you in Ukrainian, your father talks to you in Russian. Your grandad has a Polish surname, and your grandma is from St Petersburg. Your neighbour, for some reason, is Greek, and in school you have a German friend. And without even noticing it, you also become part of this place.

I never wanted to leave here. I like it here. I studied, lived, and worked here. What is Donbas for me? It's the place where I learned everything that I know. It is the place that taught me everything that I know. It is my home.

Andrii Prokopov
Mariupol, Donetsk region (occupied since 2022)

A FEW DAYS into my first visit to Mariupol, I nearly tripped over a brick. I was in the middle of an excursion around the derelict ruins of a Soviet-era industrial-machinery-building factory and there were bricks all over the place. Enterprising local residents were harvesting them from the crumbling factory walls for use in their own home-improvement projects and they were piled up in stacks everywhere you looked, waiting to be taken away in the back of someone's car. This brick that I'd almost tripped over was not just any old brick, however. This brick bore a name that was vaguely familiar: Glenboig. Having lived in Glasgow for a year when I first moved to Scotland, I had a vague memory that Glenboig was somewhere on the outskirts of the city, a road sign on the M73. Seeing its name in central Mariupol thus felt uncanny. How did this Scottish brick get here? What political or economic forces could have dropped it into my path among the post-Soviet ruins of Mariupol's manufacturing industry?

Like the salt and gypsum deposits, this brick was a portal to another world. Its presence in this metallurgy city on the Azov Sea spoke of the colonial encounters that had transformed Donbas into a fulcrum of industrial extraction by the end of the nineteenth century. This brick, I later found out, would have lined the steelmaking furnaces of a Belgian-run metallurgy factory, the capitalist predecessor of the Soviet-era machinery-building plant. Its presence in Mariupol was a result of historic profiteering by a variety of pre-revolutionary actors: the Russian Empire, which strategically welcomed foreign investment in the late 1800s; Belgian entrepreneurs, who relocated their steelmaking businesses to the region; and British brick-makers, who supplied the Belgians. What's more, as I discovered travelling round the region, this brick was one tiny piece of a much bigger puzzle. Together these pieces revealed a picture of entangled colonial modernities – the difficult legacies of which could still be felt across the heavily industrialised region.

Before Donbas became Donbas, a place synonymous with coal and extraction, it was known by another name. Located on the Pontic-Caspian Steppe, a flat grassy swathe of eastern and southern Ukraine, it formed part of the territory often referred to as the Wild Field (*dike pole* in Polish or Ukrainian, *dykra* in Lithuanian, *Loca deserta* in Latin).[1] This toponym, originating with the fifteenth-century military settlement of the steppe by Cossack armies, had gained a political charge by the 1700s. As in other 'frontier' regions of empire, it carried an idea of emptiness that was evoked by imperial actors as a justification for their colonisation of the territory. As the historian William Sunderland has noted, this fact was even reflected in etymological developments of the time. The *Dictionary of the Russian Academy* (begun 1789) thus defined a 'steppe' as 'an empty, unpopulated, and treeless place of great expanse'. It also noted that the verb 'to settle' (*zaselit'*, 'to occupy with human habitation') was best illustrated by the phrase 'to settle steppes, empty places', suggesting that steppes were territorially void, places just awaiting activation through colonisation.[2]

In reality, of course, the Wild Field was neither entirely wild nor entirely empty. Populated across time by nomadic peoples such as Tatars and Nogais, Cossacks, elite mansions, and villages in the nineteenth century, it was always an inhabited space of cultural encounter.[3] It was also an environment rich with biodiversity. The land here would blossom in early spring with delicate flowers such as cutleaf anemone, steppe irises, and pheasant's eye. In mid-May whole thickets of dark red peonies would sweep the steppe's slopes, and by mid-June a deep blue carpet of flowering sage and silvery feather grass would roll over the landscape. The Field was home to a wide

spectrum of animal life: moose, roe deer, foxes, and hares stalked its reaches, alongside slow-moving hedgehogs and scurrying ferrets. It also housed more elusive, night-time creatures such as wolves, badgers, and weasels.[4] The idea of emptiness, then, was part of the strategic mythmaking intended to justify colonisation, just as it was for the European colonisers of the American West and British settlers in Australia.

The expansion of the Russian Empire to the south, today's southeastern Ukraine, in the 1700s was driven primarily by fear. Rather than seeing the territories around the Black Sea as natural 'spaces of cultural expansion', Russia perceived this region to be a hostile, uncivilised border, inhabited by blood-thirsty enemies – the Zaporizhian Sich, the Nogai Horde, and the Crimean Khanate, a vassal of the empire's main geo-political rival, the Ottoman Empire.[5] Colonisation was a means of taming the so-called Wild Field, of bringing those 'recalcitrant' steppe communities to heel. This was no easy task, however. The military agility of the nomadic peoples posed a challenge to the empire's traditional colonial settler practices. A new tool of territorial expansion, the *zasechnaia cherta*, a heavily fortified defensive line comprising felled trees, ditches and earthen mounds and stretching hundreds of kilometres, was developed to displace the indigenous peoples from the territories.[6]

The first extension of this heavily guarded barricade into the region that would become known as Donbas took place around the salt lakes of Tor (today's Sloviansk) in the early 1700s. Salt from these lakes had for decades been extracted through solar evaporation by Zaporizhzhian Cossacks and Crimean Tatars, but at the end of the 1600s it began to attract the attention of inhabitants of the Russian Empire too.[7] Aspirational settler colonists began to journey here from Oskol and Yelets, Voronezh, Kursk and Livny, today all located in western Russia. Realising the potential for profit in these salt-rich lands, these new arrivals built defensive structures to block nomadic peoples' access to the mineral resource. In 1645, an *ostrozhek* (small fortress) was built near to a ford on the Siverskyi Donets river, where Crimean Tatars crossed to gain access to the lakes. Within twenty years, 600 soldiers from the Belgorod regiment and from other regions of the empire, along with their families, had occupied the salt-rich region.[8]

The Tor salt lakes are depicted on one of the earliest imperial maps of Ukraine, the 'Sketch of Ukrainian and Cherkassian Towns' (c. 1670). A sumptuous sepia document depicting the region's undulating rivers and networks of burgeoning villages, this sketch was created to document the territory transferred to the Muscovite Kingdom under the terms of the Andrusovo

Truce with the Polish-Lithuanian Commonwealth in 1667. In the map's upper left-hand section there is a smattering of green splodges, which might easily be passed over as either an artist's abstract rendering of treetops or unintentional ink spots. These, as Mykhailo Kulishov has demonstrated, are instead some of the earliest cartographic representations of the Tor salt lakes, unique natural landmarks of the Donetsk region.[9] The locality's mineral resources are the reason for the interest, though it is salt and not coal in this instance that has captured the colonial cartographic imagination.

In July 2021, Misha and I are driving to the Sloviansk salt lakes in search of the black-winged stilt. The uneven asphalt road along which we travel follows the contours of the lakes depicted on the seventeenth-century map. From the car I can make out bathers happily bobbing in the saline waters beneath the searing steppe sun. Pointing them out, our driver, a chatty man from Bakhmut, tells us he also likes to visit these lakes, renowned for their health-giving properties, each summer with his family. He adds that the saltwater, which oozes from the mineral-rich deposits and the gloopy mud lining the lakes' base, are a salve for skin conditions and aching joints. Soviet-era sanatoria, many of which still service Ukrainian and foreign tourists in the area, also provide other, more involved, kinds of bathing therapy. According to their purveyors, these mineral cures can help a host of health conditions, from musculoskeletal issues to gastrointestinal-tract problems.

Exiting the car, we walk down to one of the lakes that first drew the interest of Russian colonisers in the 1700s. The saltwater lies still and shallow in this area, edging a murky beach of saline mud. Humans continued to compete for control over

the mineral riches of these lands for hundreds of years after they were first colonised. The ruins of the most recent attempts to extract them for economic gain are visible nearby: a Soviet-era saltworks stands derelict, albeit still in one piece, on the banks of the lake. The abandonment of this enterprise, which Misha explains was one of many victims of the aborted economic transition after socialism, has made room for other kinds of life to return to these salty lands. The lakes, Soviet industrial ghosts and all, are now a preservation zone, protected for the black-winged stilt and other kinds of wildlife who have made them their home.

During the long and devastating Battle for Bakhmut in spring 2023, Western journalists often wondered at Russia's grim determination to gain control of such a seemingly strategically unimportant territory. But Bakhmut wasn't always strategically unimportant and perhaps never was. With the discovery in the 1700s of salt deposits even richer than those of Tor, Bakhmut quickly became a crucible of industrial production and a hub for the military on the southern border of the Russian Empire. In the first two decades of the eighteenth century, its population grew from just 150 free citizens and Cossacks in 1702 to 6,841, distributed around fourteen settlements in 1719, including entrepreneurial resettlers from the Tor and Izium salt mines who perceived better prospects for themselves in the town. When Turkish forces recaptured Azov and Taganrog, which had been seized during Peter I's Azov campaigns, Bakhmut became one of the most important military fortresses in the south of the empire. By the mid-1700s, its population, which now comprised salt miners, military personnel, artisans, and agriculturalists, had grown to around 20,000.[10]

Bakhmut, before the full-scale Russian invasion, resounded with these diverse cultural legacies. Walking around the city one balmy summer's evening with the journalist and Bakhmut native Natalia Zhukova, I was taken aback by the impressive architectural heritage of this internationally little-known city. Bakhmut remained throughout the eighteenth and nineteenth centuries a centre of trade and industry in Ukraine, acquiring the architectural accoutrements of its economic and administrative success. The wide boulevard-like streets down which I followed Natalia were lined with grand red-brick buildings built in the neoclassical and Baroque styles. As we walked, Natalia pointed out places of note – the imposing symmetrical façade of the Artemivsk Technical School of Railway Transport, the austere proportions of the Bakhmut School of Arts, both of which would be reduced to ruins by Russian bombing months later. At one point during our tour, I looked down and was surprised to see a family of hedgehogs crossing the road at my side. This indigenous species, which over many decades adapted to life on the settled steppe, would be among the many to have their lives upended when Russia escalated its military assault in 2022.

Russia's claim that Donbas has always been an integral part of the 'Russian World', and that its 'special operation' in the region was a culturally liberating one, is undone by the history of settler colonialism in this territory. Not only were the indigenous peoples of today's Donbas displaced with the expansion of empire in the 1700s, but the settler colonists who occupied the region in their wake were themselves often not ethnically Russian. As the Ukrainian historian Michael Khodarkovsky points out, the Russian Empire struggled to recruit from its Slavic peasant population to colonise what it perceived to be a dangerously underpopulated western periphery.[11] What's more, Russian and Ukrainian peasants were not always the most desirable settlers in the eyes of the empire. For the German-born Empress Catherine II (1729–96), more 'civilised' Europeans, such as German Mennonites, with their greater experience of agricultural settlement, were much more suited to the job.[12]

For this reason, following the Russo-Turkish war of 1768–74, which saw Russia wrest control of the territories on the right bank of the Dnipro river from the Crimean-Tatar state that existed between 1441 and 1783, to give the empire its desperately desired access to the Black Sea, colonisation was delivered in a surprisingly diverse range of forms. An Orthodox Hussar regiment, which on the Russian Emperor Paul III's invitation had resettled from the Austro-Hungarian Empire to the right bank of the Siverskyi Donets river and been tasked with defending the empire's border against the Turks, gives an indication of the international make-up of the population at this time. According to records, the settlement, which came to be known as Slavianoserbia, included seventy-two Serbs, twenty-two Ugric people, eleven Greeks, ten Moldavians, nine Bulgarians, three Hungarians, three Macedonians, three Turks, one Jew, one Moravian, one Russian, and one Ukrainian.[13]

The forcible incorporation of the Black Sea territories (among them parts of today's Donbas) following Catherine II's successful war against the Turks in the 1770s posed a major political challenge for the empire. This newly colonised land, which for many years had been mythologised as a realm of terroristic wilderness and depressing emptiness, now had to be marketed to potential settlers as a desirable place to make a new life. Following in the tradition of other imperial powers, such as Britain and Spain in the Americas, Catherine's answer to this challenge was to rebrand the region as Novorossiia, or 'New Russia', and to reimagine it as a natural extension of the Russian sphere of cultural influence. This process, with parallels to Russia's present war in the region, involved strategies of cultural erasure and elision that removed the toponymy and infrastructural traces of other cultural influences in these lands.[14] At the same time, a drive was begun to recruit settlers from outside of the empire's own borders in what would become a signature strategy of outsourcing colonial resettlement to foreign agriculturalists and industrialists.

Despite the name, then, 'New Russia' was far from exclusively Russian. Catherine's international advertising and strategic incentives for European settlers bore fruit in the eighteenth century with French, Dutch, English and German Mennonite communities all moving to occupy tracts of the 400,000 km² territory. Settlers were promised more land than they could ever have dreamed of back home, often bundled in with additional enticements such as ploughs, oxen, and cows, and other farming basics. Settlers received grants, which they didn't have to repay for fourteen years, and gained full ownership of their land after having cultivated it for a decade.[15] Crucially for a territory that had been violently contested for so long, foreign settlers were also exempted from military service for twenty-five years. Presented with such a desirable package, Western Europeans, and later, Ottoman dissidents (Greeks, Bulgarians, and Serbs) moved to the region in their droves.[16]

Some ethnic groups did not settle in the region of their own volition, however. Walking through the outskirts of Mariupol, where you could smell the gunpowder-like stench from the coking ovens of the distant Azovstal plant, I learned from a historian friend about the origins of the Azov Greek community. The Azov Greeks had resided in the Crimean Peninsula until Catherine's resettlement frenzy of the late 1770s. With the empire's expansion to the south and the imperial drive to populate Novorossiia with 'viable' settlers, however, they were forcibly relocated to the northern coast of the Azov Sea. Over 18,000 Greeks were resettled at this time from sixty-four towns and villages across Crimea, in what was perhaps the earliest example of forced deportation on the territory of today's Ukraine. Rather than admit to playing human chess with her imperial subjects, Catherine attempted to justify the resettlement by claiming that Orthodox Greeks were facing religious and linguistic persecution at the hands of 'Mohammedan' Crimean Tatars.[17]

Travel forwards 450 years, and Urum and Roumean, the Turkic-inflected Greek dialects spoken by the original deportees, could still be heard in the sleepy district of decorative two-storey houses through which I walked with my friend. This community still observed some of the traditions of their predecessors, cooking dishes such as plaited bread, known as chir-chir, and a meat-stuffed layer cake, kubite, on festive days, while dancing the khaitarma at local folk festivals.[18] It was impossible to think, as we wandered through the neighbourhood, that this community, whose ancestors had founded today's Mariupol, would themselves be forcibly displaced just months later. When Putin's army besieged Mariupol in 2022, Greeks were among the thousands of Mariupolites forced to flee the city by private car and minibus, and even on foot. The disingenuity of Russia's claims that it was acting in defence of persecuted Russian speakers resonated with the ethnic minority for whom similar arguments had been made to justify their colonial dispossession centuries earlier.

How, then, did settler colonialism in the Ukrainian east give way to the slow violence of industrial extraction? How did the territory known variously as the Wild Field, Slavianoserbia and Novorossiia come to be reimagined once more as Donbas?

There is a photograph in an archive in my hometown of Cardiff that holds a key to this part of the region's story. Taken by the Dowlais-born chemist Percy Cartwright, and dating from around 1910, it shows a bullock train hauling a British boiler across the snowy steppe in the direction of Hughesovka. The image speaks of the physical effort involved in industrial-ising Donbas at the turn of the century, the arduous relocation of equipment, people, and resources to the still mostly rural steppe for the purpose of excavating mineral riches – and peo-ple's fortunes – from the ground beneath. But it also speaks of the self-mythologisation of the foreign settlers as 'intrepid pioneers' to distant lands. Intentionally or not, the photograph bears a striking resemblance to Ilya Repin's celebrated painting *Barge Haulers on the Volga* (1870–73), suggesting the hardship but also the strength of spirit and fortitude of those who made the journey across the Ukrainian steppe.

The arrival of the Welsh in Hughesovka was part of a new wave of foreign settler colonialism that crashed over Donbas in the second half of the nineteenth century. Aware of its lim-itations as a largely agrarian economy, the Russian Empire introduced a series of protective fiscal measures, which, together

with the opportunities presented by new railway networks, made it more attractive to foreigners to invest in its emerging industrial markets.[19] The result was an influx of foreign capital, materials, and people into all regions of the empire, from the shipyards of St Petersburg to the metallurgy industries of the Caucasus.[20] With its extraordinary potential for industrial development, highlighted by the likes of Evhraf Kovalevskyi and other geologists, the Donets Coal Basin became a region of particular interest for foreign investors. In the decades that followed, French, Belgian, German, Dutch, British, and Russian capitalists would all play their part in extracting and exploiting the region's mineral resources, generating head-spinning amounts of profit, and in some cases losses, for industrial elites back in Western Europe and Russia.[21]

I never had the chance to visit Donetsk. By the time I started working in the east, the city had already been occupied by Russia-backed militias for two years following the occupations of 2014. Reading about the nineteenth-century Welsh settlers in the Glamorgan Archives, however, I got a peculiar sense of the place. I read letters about the difficult journeys British settlers had made to the region by boat via the Dardanelles and Bosphorus Straits, the Black Sea and Sea of Azov, before travelling, sometimes by troika, from Taganrog to Donbas. I looked at photographs of the semblances of British life that they had reconstructed for themselves on the Ukrainian steppe: the tennis courts, tea circles and amateur-dramatics clubs. Diving deeper into the archive, I learned about the worker uprisings against the British managers following accidents in the mines and outbreaks of cholera.[22] Revolution was on the horizon, though not all foreign managers could see it at that point.

Hughes's New Russia Company was registered in London in 1869 with capital of £300,000, around £28 million today, and grew exponentially over subsequent decades. By 1874 it was producing pig iron at a rate of 150 tonnes a week and rolling over 8 million kilograms of rail annually. The company built another blast furnace in 1876, along with new collieries and iron-ore mines, driving production up in the years that followed.[23] After Hughes's death in 1889, his sons expanded the company's extraction capacities, refurbishing existing furnaces and commissioning new ones, tripling iron-ore production. The expansion of the Russian Empire's railway links at the beginning of the twentieth century gave the company access to the superior ores of Kryvyi Rih, establishing Donets coal as the foundation of Russian metal manufacturing in the twentieth century. By 1910, the Ekaterinoslav governorship, in which Hughesovka was located, was producing over half of the empire's total output of coal and iron ore.[24]

By the end of the nineteenth century, over 20,000 workers and their families lived in Hughesovka. Most of these were agricultural workers from the Russian Empire who, with a shortage of land to farm, had sought alternative sources of income outside their villages.[25] The living and working conditions of the local workforce were dire. Labourers frequently lived in low-ceilinged dugouts, where tuberculosis, cholera, and dysentery were widespread.[26] British migrants, by contrast, formed a small but privileged minority. Hughes built them rows of bungalows, with alleys in between for the collection of sewage and refuse. While some of the British intermarried and became multilingual, the majority remained, until their enforced departure in 1917, an elite, gated community, who tended to regard their Ukrainian and Russian neighbours with colonial disdain.[27]

I never knew that Wales was part of the story of settler colonialism in the Russian Empire. In school we had always learned that we were the ones who were colonised by the English, who, as our history teachers explained, flooded our villages, wiped out our language, and crushed our cultural traditions. When we learned about the history of industrialisation, the emphasis was always placed on the South Wales Valleys, the pride of the working class, and Margaret Thatcher's unforgiveable closure of the mines in the 1980s, which devastated local economies and decimated communities. The story of Hughes and his company of industrial managers who journeyed to the Ukrainian steppe to make their fortunes in the late 1800s was never represented on our school curriculum. Perhaps this was because the history was less well known. Or perhaps it was felt to unhelpfully contradict Wales's understanding of itself as an economic victim of the neoliberalising British government. Either way, Hughes is still better known in Donetsk, where a statue to him – waistcoated, hammer and anvil in hand – still stands on one of the main squares, than he is in his birthplace of Merthyr Tydfil today.

Foreign capitalists settled in all parts of Donbas. Enticed by the cheap labour resulting from the emancipation of the serfs in 1861, which formally banished serfdom on the territory of the Russian Empire, and the export opportunities created by the development of the empire's railways, they moved to the region in their thousands. With the exception of Hughes in Hughesovka, British investors were primarily interested in the petroleum and gold-mining industries (58 per cent of their total investment in the Russian Empire), which drew them in the direction of the Baku oilfields in Azerbaijan and Siberia.[28] The French and Belgians, with their established expertise in heavy industry, meanwhile, were the dominant foreign investors in Donbas. The presence of Belgian capital was even more marked than that of France, which also invested heavily in the metallurgy industries of Poland and the Urals at the same time. As a result, Donbas was often referred to imperiously by European venture capitalists as 'the tenth Belgian province'.[29]

The physical transformation of the region that would become known as Donbas at the end of the nineteenth century was dramatic.[30] Between 1888 and 1900, fourteen major steel producers were built in this area, all but one of which were established with foreign investment.[31] European and Russian capitalists thought of themselves as enlightened modernisers, activating the region's 'idle resources', 'unexploited' mineral deposits and 'underemployed' labour, and driving economic progress.[32] But despite their paternalistic claims to be improving local economies and communities through the creation of work, education and welfare services, foreigner-driven industrial development was undeniably extractivist in character. In its dependence on the exploitation of local labour forces, which benefited the exporter's economy while keeping local Donbas workers in an impoverished and dependent state, it bore striking similarities to colonial managerial practices in British and French plantations, and mines in India and on the African continent. But while we are only now beginning to reckon with the history of European colonial violence in the Global South, the story of Western capital's role in resource extraction and labour exploitation in eastern Europe remains largely unknown, and thus unquestioned today.

In November 2021, three months before Russia begins its barbaric siege of Mariupol, I visit the city's massive steelworks, which were founded with foreign investment at the turn of the twentieth century. My guide this unseasonably mild winter's day is Andrii Prokopov, a workshop manager at the city's Ilych metallurgy plant, and a historical enthusiast with a passion for heavy industry. Andrii's knowledge of Mariupol's industrial past is extensive. The third generation in a line of railway workers in his family, he tells me that trainspotting is in his blood. From a fanaticism for railway heritage, Andrii's interests have gradually broadened to encompass the history of the metallurgy industries that manufactured his beloved train tracks and sleepers. As we walk, he tells me about the articles he writes for online forums and the tours he leads for other railway enthusiasts. During our four-hour excursion around the city, he talks expansively about Mariupol's industrial past, never once consulting his phone to confirm a fact or statistic, a veritable walking encyclopaedia.

Like Hughesovka, Mariupol's turn-of-the-century industries were founded partly with foreign capital. Prussian,
American, and Belgian entrepreneurs all relocated to the city
in the early 1900s, hoping to make their fortunes in the region's
emerging metallurgy markets.[33] Two such investors, brothers
Julian and Walter Kennedy, purchased and shipped to Mariupol
an entire pipe-making plant from Seattle, as well as a fully
constructed blast furnace.[34] The American-funded Nikopol'
pipe-rolling factory took orders from all over the world. Indeed,
one of its first commissions was from the British Empire for a
hundred miles of pipe to transport oil from the Baku oil fields
to mainland Europe.[35]

Around the same time, the tsarist government agreed to
allow the Belgian shareholding society Providence, which owned

numerous metallurgy factories in Belgium and France, to begin industrial production on its territory. Providence purchased land on the right bank of the Kalmius River from the Mariupol city authorities in 1897 and began building a factory, a port terminal, and iron-ore warehouses. To attract funds from other Belgian capitalists, the mangers of Providence created a new share company called Russian Providence, of which they nevertheless remained majority shareholders.[36] In 1898, the Belgians began constructing a metallurgical plant next to Nikopol' while, at the same time, laying mines in Kryvyi Rih and the surrounding area. By 1899, the plant comprised numerous furnaces and a large-scale rolling mill, which together produced thousands of tonnes of steel each year.[37] At the turn of the twentieth century, Mariupol was thus the home of two gigantic metallurgical factories and the primary producer of metal in the Russian Empire.

It's my first time in Mariupol, but I've already studied the city's sprawling factory complexes in archival photography available online.[38] Many of these images feature on turn-of-the-century postcards commissioned by foreign managers of the enterprises as corporate advertising, a showcase of the factories' most impressive assets. Postcards of the Providence factory frequently feature towering blast furnaces and smoking chimney stacks, newly laid railways lines and wagons filled to the brim with coal. Another genre of postcard shows the factory on the horizon of an otherwise undeveloped steppe landscape. The intention of such compositions is to convey a sense of utopian progress, of industrial civilisation rising Atlantis-like from the Wild Field. Looking now, from a moment of heightened ecological consciousness, the images strike a more melancholic note, revealing a hubristic, shortsighted belief in the progressive nature of industrial modernity.

A striking example of this genre of postcard, dating from the 1910s, shows a romantic figure glancing back at the photographer against the sepia backdrop of the factory. Andrii wants to show me where this photograph – now much reproduced in local exhibitions and publications – was taken, so we speed off in his car in the direction of the river. We get out in an inauspicious spot on the hard shoulder of a busy five-lane motorway. Andrii holds up the image: the expansive steppe, which divides the figure in the foreground from the factory complex behind, is now a sprawling district of urban housing, shops, service stations and roads. Behind us, in the direction the figure is gazing, is the Ilych metallurgy works. In the view before us today it seems almost entirely unchanged from those postcards. The chaotic assemblage of dirty rusting warehouses, blast furnaces, chimneys, and pipes forms a timeless composition. White smoke billows from pipes behind the high concrete wall, next to which a row of sorry-looking, spindly trees have been planted, presumably as toxic-wind breaks.

Having gazed upon the industrial monolith that is the Ilych steelworks for some minutes and drawn its fumes into our lungs, Andrii suggests that we get a breath of fresher air at the now ruined site of the former Providence factory. A ten-minute car journey later and we pull up at the entranceway to what was, not so long ago, the Azovmash plant, a Soviet-era enterprise that specialised in building military equipment, constructing missile tanks, rocket launchers, and armoured vehicles. Passing through the ceremonious entranceway, which still bears the enterprise's name in an italicised 1980s

font and its logo of intersecting component parts, we enter a vast and derelict complex. Andrii tells me he likes to come to this atmospheric site to ponder Mariupol's complicated industrial legacies and challenging present. He gestures at me to follow him inside and begins to stride down a rubble-strewn road along which vehicles transporting industrial products must once have thundered. Beneath the heavy, grey November sky, all is eerily quiet, aside from birdsong and the occasional banging of brick and metal collectors at work.

Azovmash was built in 1958 on the base of what was at that time the machine-building section of the Zhdanov metallurgy works named after Ilych. Ilych itself was a reincarnation of the Belgian-run Providence plant, which had been nation-alised and purged of its foreign capitalist managers following the Bolshevik Revolution in 1917. The plant, renamed after Lenin, whose patronymic was Ilych, had become a top-secret laboratory for manufacturing armoured steel in the 1930s. It was here that Mariupol cast armour was first developed, from which parts for the Soviets' famous T–34 tanks were made during World War II.[39]

After the war, the plant began to adapt its production to the needs of a peacetime Soviet economy and to manufacture agricultural machinery and metallurgy equipment. Later, when the government became consumed with winning the space race and asserting its technological superiority over the West, it received orders to manufacture fuel-supply equipment that would be used in every Soviet space rocket, including Yuri Gagarin's. With the collapse of the Soviet Union in 1991 and the disappearance of state defence orders, the factory entered a period of protracted economic decline. Sections of the enterprise began to be asset-stripped and sold off for parts by new owners. As the plant fell into dereliction, the metal and brick collectors moved in, accelerating the destruction. As we walk around the complex, we see several of these industrious tradespeople at work, deconstructing walls with sledgehammers and loading bricks, wire, and other saleable materials into parked cars.

Andrii holds up a printout of a turn-of-the-century postcard photograph of the Providence factory. The before-and-after effect is impressive. The steppe that was transformed one hundred years ago into a crucible of mineral extraction and labour exhaustion is turning back into steppe; the pioneer trees and horsetail grasses are taking root, reclaiming this landscape as their own. This is no romantic story of environmental rebirth and renewal, however. Just months after our visit, following the siege and occupation of the city, I read stories of the derelict complex being strewn with missiles and grenade launchers and of it being mined by Ukrainian soldiers as they retreated from the city. This place, which had been so many things already – Providence, Ilych, Azovmash – is now entering a new phase of its turbulent history under Russian occupation. The Scottish brick that I'd tripped over, the portal into this complicated and multi-layered past, presumably remains there today, now among other deadlier and more toxic kinds of rubble.

Donbas before 1917 was a knot of colonial entanglements. It was a colonial 'contact zone' in the realest sense of the term, a contested social space where, as the literary scholar Mary Louise Pratt has put it, 'cultures meet, clash, and grapple with each other ... in highly asymmetrical relations of power'.[40] Empress of Russia Catherine II's settler colonialism of the 1700s, which sought to displace indigenous peoples from the newly colonised Black Sea territories and replace them with loyal, multi-ethnic imperial subjects, paved the way in the eighteenth century for the flourishing of foreigner-funded extractivist colonialism. The Hugheses and the Kennedys, who extracted the region's mineral riches and exploited local workforces for their own economic gain, may not have been settler colonists in the traditional sense, but their economic activities were undoubtedly colonial in nature.

This knotty history has left its mark on the region's communities and its landscapes, as I discover during a separate excursion with Misha Kulishov. Early one morning in 2021, before the July heat has fully claimed the day, we visit a railway intersection near Bakhmut called Stoupky. I follow Misha as he crosses the railway tracks and picks his way through the knee-high grass, arriving at a deep pond bordered by thick foliage and thistles. This, he explains, is the spot on which a Dutch salt mine stood until 1944, though it ceased mining twenty years before that.[41] Two decades of slow flooding of the mined cavities beneath the ground have formed a sinkhole fifty metres across and forty metres deep. As we crouch by its side and gaze down at the opaque water, Misha tells me about divers who have brought up from its depths remnants of the mine's Dutch decorative architecture and metal. It's an underwater archive of colonial encounter and industrial expansion.

The submerged Dutch salt mine at the bottom of the sinkhole in Stoupky seems a powerful metaphor for the purposeful forgetting of what formed state policy in Ukraine following the Bolshevik Revolution in 1917. Once the communists had consolidated power in this region, they set about erasing the cultural memory of the era of European capitalist investment, renaming factories and settlements and even removing archives to Moscow and Leningrad. In the 1930s, an alternative origin myth was created for Donbas that held that the Georgian first secretary Joseph Stalin was single-handedly responsible for the industrial transformation and modernisation of the region. As we wander around the sinkhole, getting scratched and covered in burrs, I talk to our driver, Vladyslav, who lives in a village not far from Stoupky, about the Dutch salt miners Cornelius Terven and Dirk Van der Made, who made their fortunes extracting salt here over a hundred years ago. Vladyslav tells me that this is the first he's heard about the curious story, and that he doesn't know anyone from the area who doesn't also think the region was founded in the 1930s by the Soviets.

Before Russia's full-scale invasion in 2022, cultural activists were working to bring this complicated history of entangled colonialisms to broader audiences in Donbas. Enthusiasts of the region's industrial history, like Misha and Andrii, journalists like Natalia, museum workers, archivists, and filmmakers, were beginning to excavate this hidden story and explore its resonances for today's Ukraine. Speaking with people about this chapter in the region's past, I could feel their desire to imagine another Donbas, a place rich in cultural encounters, much more than an industrialised periphery of the so-called 'Russian World'. With Russia's occupation of this territory, however, these activities have been brought to a halt. Museums have been looted and activists displaced. The history that was emerging from the archives has once more disappeared from view. But, as divers and archivists know, you can't hide the past at the bottom of a sinkhole. There will always be a curious few who will dive to the bottom, determined to bring its remnants to the surface.

THREE

Cults

My family moved to Mariupol in 1992 when I was fifteen years old. But before that we used to come here on our summer holidays, from the early 1980s onwards. For me, the city will always be associated with food. Everything in Mariupol was such good quality: the special kinds of dumplings, lemon cake, buckets of apricots. Mariupol's shops were always well stocked in comparison to other cities. I could stand in all of the most interesting queues and, with my eyes closed, distinguish a Rusanivs'ka sausage from a Ostankins'ka one. I also remember the bookshop Azovstalets, where, growing up, I bought all my favourite books – mostly about geography and biology. And for the record, I never once saw a single book there about the Azovstal factory or the metallurgy industry.

One of my favourite walks in Mariupol, a very personal one for me, is along the Pishchanka beach. This is the place I would always walk with the people and thoughts that were most important to me. I have already charged this place with such magnetic energy, or rather romanticised it, that I'll probably return to it even after I die. Thirty-metre-high sandstone cliffs and the most beautiful bee-eater birds in the air, labyrinths of boathouses, people hiding from the busy central beaches – this is my Mariupol Mediterranean, a tremendously important landscape that brings the city close to the lyrical prose of Cesare Pavese.

Another walk that I'll never forget is along the highway from the Left Bank, where I lived, to the city centre. This road skirts the edge of the factory for about five kilometres, following the monolithically grey factory wall. I've walked down this highway dozens of times, travelled along it by tram thousands of times, and driven down it by marshrutka taxi hundreds of thousands of times, and this wall is a powerful metaphor for my relationship with the city. I used to think that painting it could be like the fall of the Berlin Wall for Mariupol.

Later, an artist from Mariupol explained to me that the Azovstal wall could and should always remain grey. Since then, it has functioned like a kind of industrial meditation for me. A nothing that is nothing.

Sashko Protyah

Mariupol, Donetsk region (occupied since 2022)[1]

IN KYIV'S bustling Solomianskyi district there is a quiet, pigeon-filled courtyard that holds some of the country's most important historical documents. The State Central Historical Archive and the Pshenychnyi Audio-Visual Archive can be reached by following a trail of handmade signs mounted in plastic envelopes and taped to trees that take you around a maze of paths across the square. In the winter of 2021, I visited Pshenychnyi with the idea of consulting the archive's collection of industrial-worker portrait photography. I was interested in viewing the portraits of Stakhanovites, the Soviet Union's prized industrial workers, who were awarded special status and material benefits for overfulfilling their quotas at work. My topic seemed to me niche, so I was surprised when the archivist, a serious person in western Ukrainian national dress, listened without a flicker of surprise to my request and then disappeared into the stacks. Minutes later, she reappeared carrying boxes heaving with portrait photographs of the Soviet state's most prodigious miners and steelworkers. 'These are just the Donbas photographs from the 1930s,' she told me, her tone matter-of-fact, 'and there are twenty or so more boxes from that decade once you are done with this lot.'

In the first two decades of Soviet rule, Donbas became a flagship region of Soviet hyper-productivity and its labourers the poster boys and girls of communist propaganda. Its industrial achievements were celebrated in documentary films and monumental murals, displayed at exhibitions of technological prowess, and commemorated in the national press. Worker cults, some of which reached levels comparable to global celebrity today, were an important part of the Soviet mythologisation of Donbas. By the end of the 1930s, everyone knew about the superhuman feats of the Horlivka miner, Mykyta Izotov, who hewed 240 tonnes of coal in one shift, thirty times his allocated quota, and Oleksii Stakhanov, from the Central-Irmino mine in Kadiivka, who smashed Izotov's record in 1935.[2] What's more, the regime succeeded in communicating to people across the multinational empire that Izotov and Stakhanov's models were ones to be emulated and admired. The boxes and boxes of portraits of coal-streaked miners and sinewy steelworkers at Pshenychnyi are material traces of this hyper-extractivist ideology that had gripped the country by the late 1930s.

It may at first seem strange that a political regime like the Soviet Union, so invested in the romantic ideal of the workers' collective, would make celebrities out of individual labourers. It might appear equally odd that this declaredly anti-materialist society awarded these individuals such ostentatious prizes as sewing machines, watches, gramophones, and motorbikes for their efforts. But as I flicked through images of Soviet hero labourers in the boxes at Pshenychnyi, it became clear these cults were meant to incentivise people into investing ever more of themselves into the project of building Soviet industrial modernity. By heaping praise on individual labourers, they were also meant to compensate for more serious shortcomings in the organisation of society and the economy. Reading more in the periodicals and history books housed at Kyiv's archives and libraries about the turbulent years in Donbas that had followed the 1917 Revolution, I discovered why such symbolic gestures had become necessary. How, in those decades of political upheaval, dramatic societal transformation, and rapid infrastructural growth, photographs of miners being effusively thanked with bouquets of flowers became essential tools of social control.

◈

Lenin has seldom rested easy on his pedestal in Ukraine. There have always been those eager to knock him down, string him up, or simply bury him in the ground. This became more obvious than ever during Ukraine's Revolution of Dignity. Following the mass protests in the capital that resulted from the brutal dispersion of peacefully protesting students on Independence Square in November 2013, a wave of monument-toppling began that came to be known as *Leninopad* or Leninfall.[3] Starting with a rose-marbled Lenin located across the road from Kyiv's Bessarabia Market – already a source of debate from the 1990s following the removal of a much larger Lenin from Kyiv's main square – effigies of the Bolshevik leader began to be felled across the country.[4] Though tolerance for communist symbolism was greater in heavily industrialised Donbas, where Soviet insignia were more tightly interwoven into the urban fabric, in the early months of 2014 Lenins started to tumble in the east as well.[5] Whether pulverised by angry activists or buried in back gardens by panicking communists, Lenins disappeared from Kostiantynikva to Mariupol in the early months of 2014. Many of the disgraced monuments left behind them empty pedestals, which you would find in parks and on street corners when wandering through the cities, the future function of which came to be hotly debated by local communities.

Decommunisation, the process of systematically removing the cultural heritage of the Soviet era from public spaces in Ukraine, accelerated in 2015. As Russia annexed the Crimean Peninsula and launched its hybrid military campaign in the Donbas region, freshly elected President Poroshenko adopted the furthest-reaching measures in history to purge the country of its communist heritage and socialist toponymy.[6] Disentangling the industrial infrastructure that dominated the Ukrainian east from the cultural influence of communism, however, proved a fraught and occasionally emotionally triggering task. While Lenin monuments had fallen easily in some places, the renaming of factories, streets, and cities proved more controversial for those who'd grown up working, living, and having their most formative social experiences in and around these places.

The centrally enforced decommunisation laws elicited some subversive responses in the Ukrainian east. Familiar communist names were smuggled back in during the renaming processes, at times to humorous effect. Artemivsk, named after the Bolshevik revolutionary and contemporary of Stalin, Feder Sergeev, aka Artem, may thus have shed its communist chrysalis to emerge as Bakhmut in 2015, but the ghost of Artem still lingered in the ambiguously renamed champagne factory, ArtWinery.[7] Likewise, as the director of the Ilych Iron and Steelmaking Museum in Mariupol explained when I visited in 2021, the factory's problematic association with Vladimir Ilych Ulyanov, aka Vladimir Lenin, had ostensibly been resolved by excavating another Ilych from the region's past and transferring the credit for the factory's name to them.[8] The fact that Ilych was run by Metinvest, a company owned by one of Ukraine's foremost oligarchs, Rinat Akhmetov, no doubt may also have helped deflect public criticism in this case of disingenuous decommunisation.

If decommunisation was a vexed process in the east, the original process of communisation had not been much easier. Much to Lenin's chagrin, the workers of Donbas – who should have been the perfect soil in which the Bolshevik proletarian-led ideology could take root – had not responded as they should to the call to revolution. This was partly due to the suspicions workers harboured towards managers of any political ilk.[9] Following years of exploitation at the hands of foreign co-owners of local industries – the Hugheses, the Farkes, and the Kennedys – who had varnished their exploitative enterprises with paternalistic patinas, labourers in Donbas were understandably disinclined to trust any virtue-signalling manager. Rather than manifesting a defined class identity, then, as Lenin would have wished, workers were preoccupied with more immediate and pressing problems such as food and soap shortages, fatal accidents at work, and poor housing provision.[10]

The years that followed the Bolshevik Revolution were incredibly difficult. Workers in Donbas were subjected to extremes of violence as the region changed hands repeatedly between the communist 'Reds', the monarchist 'Whites', and the anarchist 'Blacks' across the tumultuous years of the Russian Civil War (1917–22). Labourers wisely refused to identify with any ideology during this time of total societal upheaval. Indicative of the political unpredictability of this period was the glass-making town of Kostiantynivka, which reportedly changed hands twenty-seven times during the chaotic months between February and May 1919.[11] As with the war ongoing in Donbas today, local communities and urban infrastructure experienced the worst of the violence resulting from the political conflict, violence that also triggered mass displacement, which came to be known as 'the great migration of peoples'. The devastation of the region by the mid-1920s was almost complete. As one Bolshevik travelling through Donbas in December 1919 wrote, this 'economic centre of the Soviet Republic' had become a 'Donbas cemetery of miners and steelworkers'.[12] As the war raged on, industrial workers fled in their droves.

❖

At the Pshenychnyi Audio-Visual Archive in Kyiv I am handed an album of photographs of workers from Yenakiieve, a currently occupied mining town around sixty kilometres north-west of Donetsk. The photographs were produced for a commemorative album, *The Launch of the Yenakiieve Plant (1924–1925)*, celebrating the reopening of the metallurgy factory in the years following the Civil War.[13] Factory launches were a popular theme of early Soviet photo-chronicles. The recommencement of industrial production was given as evidence of renewed political stability, a visual manifestation of the Bolshevik victory over the Whites and Blacks. To mark the symbolic significance of this occasion, a professional photographer had been dispatched from Kyiv to create images that would be circulated around the country in newspapers. One of the most striking photos in the collection is a group portrait of workers posing next to an enormous blast furnace. The image recalls pre-revolutionary corporate photography, in which anonymous labourers were included in industrial landscapes to illustrate scale. Here too we are supposed to wonder at the awesome power of industry, its resilience and its potential to transform.[14]

The Yenakiieve album contains another curious photograph. The image is a studio portrait of four technical engineers gathered around a model of a blast furnace. The men have been placed by the photographer in unnaturally symmetrical poses. The two seated subjects cross their outer legs, causing their toes to touch, while the men standing behind them grasp the chair backs, making their arms bow like handles on a Grecian vase. The men look far from at ease. Standing stiffly and engulfed in their ill-fitting finery, they recall August Sander's photograph of three farmers on their way to a dance, who, as John Berger noted, present a visual anachronism in their fancy suits.[15] The men in this portrait are visually incongruous in a different way. Their selection for this image is symbolic: it is no longer just the managers of labour who are worthy of depiction, it suggests, but also those skilful technicians on whom production relies. The inclusion of the model blast furnace in this photo is revealing. So large and dominating in the first photograph, it appears here as a much smaller-scale model, almost like a toy. Rather than machinery assigning identity to the industrial workers, it is the workers who are now pictured as the masters of the industrial machinery.

I was never able to visit Yenakiieve. By the time I started my research in Donbas, it was already in the zone occupied by Russian-backed separatists from 2014. I had heard about it, though, of course. Yenakiieve is known to every Ukrainian, and to everyone who works on Ukraine, as the hometown of the notorious pro-Russian former president, Viktor Yanukovych, who was so spectacularly ousted from power following the Maidan Revolution in 2014. Yanukovych had in fact begun his professional life at the metallurgy works

depicted in these photographs. A qualified mechanical engineer, his first post at the age of nineteen in 1969 had been as a gas worker at the Yenakiieve plant. This was deep in the era of Leonid Brezhnev – the Soviet leader who followed Nikita Khrushchev in 1964 – that was characterised by political stagnation and economic decline, when corruption was rife and political fortunes were made via crime and professional networks.[16] Yanukovych was one such beneficiary of this broken system, ascending the greasy pole of politics via senior managerial positions at Donbas-based production firms, and the Donetsk Regional Administration, before becoming Governor of the Donetsk Region in 1997–2002 and, after that, the Prime Minister of Ukraine under Leonid Kuchma in 2002. Along this journey, Yanukovych reportedly amassed vast amounts of personal and party capital by asset-stripping, embezzlement, and other forms of corruption.[17] His eye-watering wealth was evidenced when activists broke into his Mezhyhiria estate after he fled to Rostov-on-Don. The obscene luxury of the estate, which included a faux galleon on the waterfront and a collection of exotic animals, was a dark mirror world to the defunded and dismembered architecture of socio-economically destitute Yenakiieve in the east.[18]

❧

The makers of *The Launch of the Yenakiieve Plant* photo album had good cause to celebrate. The civil war had dealt a terrible blow to industrial production in the east: at the beginning of 1920, none of the sixty-five blast furnaces that had operated to full capacity in 1913 was working, and by 1921 over half of the industrial plants in Donbas had closed.[19] On the brink of economic collapse, the Soviet government had introduced harsh measures to increase its productivity. Coal mining was militarised: Red Army soldiers were brought in to supplement the dwindling labour force; mobility was restricted to curb seasonal migration; and war prisoners, including Don Cossacks, who had fought against the Bolsheviks during the civil war, were made to do forced labour in the mines. These dire conditions, combined with famine caused by economic ruin, grain acquisition and drought, drove people to despair. If the Bolsheviks had been appalled by the lack of collective worker consciousness in Donbas in 1917, their catastrophic policies had now delivered this at their own expense: in 1923 more than 200 strikes swept the region, with over 60,000 local labourers taking part.[20]

Things would get no better in Donbas once Stalin came to power. Despite having played a leading role in the coordination of the oil workers' strikes in Baku in 1909 and 1910, Lenin's successor had no mercy for Donbas's striking labourers, whom he accused of being destructive enemies of the people. For Stalin, the fact that Donbas had become a magnet for migrant workers following the recovery of industry in the region was a cause for particular concern. As he saw it, the influx of starving peasants, fleeing their famine-stricken villages to find work in nearby factories, and politically disgraced engineers and technical specialists, seeking to disappear into the Ukrainian steppe, created conditions ripe for political dissent.[21] As the dictator's persecution complex increased across the 1920s, attacks on these 'suspicious' groups intensified. Things came to a head in Donbas in 1928, when fifty-three engineers and managers from the coal-mining town of Shakhty (today located across the border in Russia) were tried for conspiracy to sabotage the Soviet economy.[22] The Shakhty Affair would become the Soviet Union's first major show trial.

Labour exhaustion, famine, poverty, persecution: these are some of the realities that hover behind the portraits of Stakhanovites that fill the boxes at Pshenychnyi Archive. Some images of celebrated quota-busting workers from the 1930s visually gesture at these hardships. An unevenly framed photograph of a stoker named D. Diakonov from the No. 10 Artem mine in Voroshilovgrad (today's Luhansk) shows a man whose skin seems leathered by his work tending the industrial furnace, his eyes screwed up against the sun. Two more portraits jump out at me of women Stakhanovites, both from a collective farm in the Kostiantynivka region. The two women look directly at the camera, their gaze intense and probing. Knowing the hunger and fear that communities in Donbas villages and cities experienced at this time, it is hard not to project desperate meaning onto their expressions.

The archivist brings me out another box of hero-labourer portrait photographs. Hours have passed and I'm only just at the end of the 1930s. By this time the state-sponsored Stakhanovite movement was in full swing. Stalin would have had people believe that this was a grassroots initiative, something that had spontaneously sprung from the *narod*, the people, and their love for and commitment to the project of building communism. In reality, it was entirely state manufactured. As historian Lewis Siegelbaum explains, Oleksii Stakhanov was selected by his local party cell to take up the challenge of mining over a

hundred tonnes of coal in one shift. The record-breaking act had been staged at 10 p.m., after the normal working day, and rewarded with a prize of 200 roubles instead of the twenty-three to thirty roubles that a miner would have normally received for their efforts.[23] But it was less the record itself than the hype that followed it that propelled the movement. Stakhanov was adopted by the party as a celebrity and paraded around the Soviet Union, giving speeches, shaking hands with delegates. He even featured on the cover of *Time* magazine in December 1935 – a surprising fact that reveals the United States's interest at this time in emerging Soviet cults.

The Stakhanov cult resulted in 'record mania' (*rekordsmenstvo*) sweeping the USSR.[24] With prizes, privileges, and press photographs up for grabs, workers strove to beat their quotas in industrial sectors from lens-making to engine-building. And, to begin with at least, it was not hard to achieve the official status of Stakhanovite. With outdated production quotas that had not yet caught up with the mechanisation of industry in some sectors, labourers easily smashed their targets. Indeed, bizarrely, quota-smashing became so common that by July 1940, 3 million Soviet labourers (around half of the total workforce) had achieved the revered status.[25] The value of the accolade must have seemed questionable to some. And no wonder it was taking me so long to get through these boxes of photos.

The archivist comes back after her lunch and asks me if I've had a chance to look through the list of films about Donbas Stakhanovites that they have at the archive. It turns out that the communist state was just as keen on documenting their hero labourers on film as they were on capturing them in photographs. I select some intriguing titles from the list for viewing. The reels are beautifully vintage: rusting metal covers with rose-coloured labels featuring Soviet-era fonts and neat, neat archival handwriting. My archive fever ramps up when we get to the room for private viewings. This room houses an epoch-defining, open-topped Soviet film deck that would not be out of place in a museum of Cold War history. Much to my delight, it is in perfect working order. On the command of the archivist, the film flickers into life and time-warped sound.

The images on screen show Stakhanov at his record-breaking work.[26] By the late 1980s, when this film was made, audiences must have been sick of this overzealous miner whose model they were still supposed to diligently follow. Stakhanov himself appears in the film, slightly wooden and awkward, but remarkably photogenic. The montage moves from dynamic shots of him underground with his signature drill to more wholesome scenes of him, now adorned in a crisp *vyshyvanka*, writing letters at a surprisingly luxurious writing desk, bust of Lenin at its helm. From here the film moves on to more scenes of healthful and happy life in the industrial region: nursery-school expeditions to the green and leafy parks around the mines and performances of high-heeled women in dance ensembles, dressed in spotless white in front of enraptured cross-legged audiences. Being a Stakhanovite was not just about coal on scales, the film informs us. It was also about performing 'culturedness', being an ideal Soviet citizen inside *and* outside the factory or mine.[27]

The Stakhanovite movement was the literal smiling face of the Stalin-era terror. As 'bourgeois' specialists and suspected dissidents were hunted down by the merciless state machine, these worker heroes were heralded as the country's future, examples of the emerging class of New Soviet Men and Women who would lead the USSR to communism. These men and women, it was claimed, would be the ones to step up and take over the reins of government once the 'revolutionary vanguard' – a temporary fix, in any case – was no longer necessary. Unlike academicians, who never got their hands dirty, Stakhanovites, with their hard-earned practicality, rationality, and their inherent, unshakeable love of and loyalty to the communist cause, were the natural heirs to the Soviet throne.

This was the theory, at least. The reality, of course, was much more cynical. Many Stakhanovites were discarded when they could serve no further purpose for the production-fixated regime. This was the case for the most famous and original Stakhanovite. When Nikita Khrushchev decided in 1957 that Oleksii Stakhanov had served his purpose in boosting the labour-production movement, he returned him to his native Donbas – where he apparently felt himself in virtual exile. He is said to have spent the next twenty years drinking heavily and pondering the strange fate that had befallen him.²⁸ That chapter in his story is, of course, nowhere to be found among the images and films housed at Pshenychnyi.

Two weeks later and I'm being introduced to a very local history of Stakhanovism at the Ilych Iron and Steelmaking Museum in Mariupol. I am on an excursion with Iryna Badasen, the museum's authoritative director, who is using a Soviet-style pointing stick that she's decorated with diamanté stickers and tassels to show me items of socialist-era industrial memorabilia. The stick points at portraits of overproducing heroes of labour, dioramas of blast furnaces and steelworks, and propaganda posters of overalled metalworkers hauling red-hot steel from baking ovens. I have always been fascinated by these company-sponsored industrial museums, which exist in many factories and plants across the eastern region. Despite the decommunisation laws, these privately run institutions have remained stuck in time, a product of the proletarian cult that colonised thinking here for almost seventy years.

The museum is located on the gated territory of the Ilych factory complex and can be reached only by passing through a monumental entryway bearing the name of the Ukrainian oligarch Rinat Akhmetov's steel and mining group, Metinvest. On both sides of the ceremonial gates are portraits of steelworkers: to the left, a half-smiling steelworker from 1897, the year of the plant's foundation by American financiers; to the right, a colour portrait of a robust-looking welder, depicted against a backdrop of fiery metallic orange, from 2017. The symbolism of the composition is straightforward: those passing through the entryway are invited to imagine themselves as part of a

long history of industrial labour, following in a proud tradition. Despite the bluntness of the iconography, walking between the two images, like sphynxes marking the entrance to some mythical world, feels like a rite of passage. I have the sense of having left one Mariupol realm and entered another.

Being inside the gated complex is an uncanny experience. Things look broadly the same here – same architectural styles, same street decorations, same asphalt – but everything is in a slightly better condition: not so many potholes, more evenly laid paving slabs, freshly painted railings. What's more, while Metinvest's presence can be felt everywhere in the city, its symbolism here is omnipresent. I walk past billboards that speak exclusively of the factory's achievements, its pioneering technology, its leadership, and its paternalistic care for its employees. At the end of one road, I stop to photograph a stand displaying the names and images of today's Stakhanovites. The words at the top of the stand, between the Metinvest logos, read

'Our Pride'. Below are columns of photographs of the factory's most exceptional employees. All bar two of the twenty are men.

In the Soviet period, a stand such as this would have been called a 'Board of Honour' (*doska pocheta*). You would encounter them in workplaces, such as the Ilych Steel and Iron Works, but also in schools, clubs, museums, and on village squares.[29] Not entirely dissimilar to the 'Employee of the Month' portraits hanging on the walls of a McDonald's, these boards were vehicles of social engineering. Employees, it was hoped, would strive to fulfil their potential, to have their images symbolically displayed alongside other local heroes of socialist labour. Where the Soviet tradition departed from capitalist motivational practices, however, was in its espousal of the board of honour's darker counterpart, the 'Board of Shame' (*doska pozora*).[30] This stand would typically show images of inadequate workers: 'slackers', 'shirkers', 'boozers', and 'parasites'. This kind of public shaming through photography does at least seem to have since been discarded at the company today.

Ilych was founded on the post-revolutionary ruins of the foreign-financed Nikopol pipe-rolling factory. Following the expulsion of the reviled foreign capitalists, the enterprise's name was changed, Soviet legend has it, by popular demand. Workers are said to have gathered at the factory's entryway on a frosty January morning in 1924, two days after Lenin's death, to demand that Factory A, as it was then known, be rechristened Ilych in honour of their secular saint. The factory's significance in the economic system of Soviet production grew in line with its prestigious namesake. As demand for pipes soared with the development of the Soviet oil and shipbuilding industries, workers in all sectors, from furnace stokers to metal rollers, had to produce wares at an ever-faster pace.[31]

Before Stakhanovism was even a term, overproduction was a state expectation. Before Stakhanov, there were 'strike workers' (in Russian *udarnik*, from the word *udar*, meaning a strike or blow with a hammer) and there is a whole gallery of them on show at the Ilych Museum. I have already followed my knowledgeable guide through several rooms, all heaving with historical exhibits relating to the factory's tumultuous experiences during the revolution and civil war. The bearded faces of paternalistic Belgian and American managers have come and gone in the museum's well-polished vitrines, and we have finally arrived at a board entitled *Udarnichestvo* – 'Strike Work'. Iryna stops here to tell me about the feats of labour that early Soviet workers at the Ilych plant undertook to elevate the enterprise's production and set an example for the rest of the country. Not content to follow the general trend of fulfilling the First Five Year Plan (Stalin's industrial Great Leap Forward) in four years, Mariupol workers wanted to do it in three, she explains.

Why would the exhausted and exploited hewers and stokers of Donbas have wanted to support this ideological movement? Was it coercion, political fervour, slavish obedience, boredom, or some mixture of all these things? Iryna's pointing stick directs my attention to a statistic on one of the boards. In June 1930, 9,600 workers at the Mariupol factory received the status of strike worker . . . 9,600![32] Strike working was such a phenomenon at Ilych that that the factory was celebrated as the pride of the black metallurgy industry of Ukraine, and overachieving workers were awarded prizes totalling 200,000 roubles (nearly $2 million today), she says. With local patriotism that has not been tempered by the decommunisation laws, Iryna adds that the factory was awarded a Red Banner of the All-Union Central Council of Trade Unions in 1930. This was the highest honour a factory could receive at the time.

Iryna moves me along to a cast-iron bust of a young man vaguely resembling James Dean. The man's high cheekbones and strong jawline, slightly raised as he gazes intently towards the horizon, make him an archetypal New Soviet Man.[33] This is Makar Mazai, the primo Stakhanovite of Mariupol's Ilych metallurgy works. Mazai was a steelworker at the open-hearth shop and became the face of Mariupol's famed 'accelerated steel-making movement'.[34] It is hard for most of us to imagine the physically demanding work of tending an open-hearth furnace. Furnace stokers hauled molten metal into and out of an insatiable fiery mouth for hours on end, monitoring the chemical reactions that took place to sustain a river of red-hot steel that flowed from the holes drilled into the oven's side.

Accelerating this skilled and hazardous work to achieve the formerly unheard-of levels of production realised by Makar in the 1930s seems deeply risky – and reckless, even. In the Stalin-era cult of ubiquitous overproduction, however, it was celebrated as an exemplary patriotic exploit.

Like Stakhanov, Mazai's post-mortem cult in Mariupol came to be even more important than his original feat of labour overproduction. The many exhibits on display at the museum, to which Iryna now directs my attention, attest to this fact. One stand is packed with photos of Mazai's descendants, both literal and figurative. Alongside photographs of his children and grandchildren, standing awkwardly in their Sunday best near a roaring furnace, are photographs of Mazai's modern-day 'followers' (*posledovateli*): smiling steelworkers in padded jackets and flip-down protective goggles, the style of which has changed little from the 1930s. A nearby clothes stand is adorned with the items worn by decorated steelworkers who trod in the hallowed footsteps of the Mariupol Stakhanovite. The faded orange banner draped over a steelworker's padded jacket reads '60 years of Mazai's Record!' Worn by some prodigious steelworker just a year before the collapse of the Soviet project in 1991, this may have been the last formal celebration of the locally acclaimed hero of labour.

Iryna is an exemplary excursion guide: authoritative, engaging, but also able to crack a joke when the occasion calls for it. Her usual crowd is steelworkers and visiting groups from local towns and villages in the Donetsk region. Since the museum opened in the 1960s, new employees have visited the display as part of their induction into working life at the plant. While the main exhibition has changed little since the Soviet period, two new rooms have been added in recent years, one of which commemorates the life and work of the factory's most beloved post-Soviet director, Volodymyr Boiko. I have already encountered several effigies of Boiko during my short time in the city. His benevolent smile beams down from billboards on the sides of sports centres and shopping precincts, while various streets and highways bear his name, particularly within the factory district. Here at the museum, something almost shrine-like has been constructed in his honour. It is into this *pièce de résistance* that Iryna now gestures that we enter.

Anthropologists would say that Boiko was a typical *khaziain*. The word translates variously as 'master', 'owner', 'boss' or 'man of the house' but in the context of post-Soviet labour relations

and patronage networks refers to a manager's role as provider of welfare and social care and, crucially, to their rootedness in the local community.[35] Calling to mind descriptions of paternalistic managers such as John Hughes in the late nineteenth century, Boiko is described in the anniversary publication *The Heart of Ukrainian Metallurgy*, which Iryna presents me with at the end of our tour, as 'a real man: strict but fair, demanding of others and of himself' and that while capable of strong words and strict management, he never turned into a tyrant, remaining until his death 'a director of the people'.[36]

It is easy to understand why Boiko is so popular in Mariupol. Under his management, the factory built the prestigious Ilychevets sports stadium, restored the city's theatre, provided gas to deprived working-class districts, founded schools, nurseries and community centres, and extended tram and trolleybus networks. Boiko understood the unspoken rules of the social contract between *khaziains* and their dependants. The loyalty of one's subjects did not come for free, but had to be earned or, in some cases, even bought. The factory might demand everything from its labourers, working them to the point of physical exhaustion, but in exchange it would ensure that shops were well stocked and that roads were pothole-free. After Boiko, Iryna tells me, this relationship broke down. The new director did not respect the rules of the game and pursued labour exhaustion without its usual rewards. The result was simmering resentment and frustration among the city's working-class communities.

The Boiko exhibit, I must admit, gives me the creeps. An exact reconstruction of the deceased director's office, it comprises

Boiko's intimate personal possessions: satchel, suit jacket, calculator, even an open cigarette packet. While the cigar resting in the ashtray and the coat slung over the back of the chair suggest Boiko has just stepped out of the room for a moment, the whole composition, positioned on a diagonal and including archival documents that form an awning across the scene, reminds us that this is indeed a museum set. Within the installation there is a second commemorative object: a portrait of the director crafted from shards of amber, which was gifted by local workers to their 'talented manager' in recognition of a prominent anniversary in 2003. Recalling the historian Jeffrey Brooks's argument about practices of gift-giving to Stalin as expressions of the people's immeasurable indebtedness to the Soviet leadership, this portrait seems further to affirm Boiko's *khaziain* status.[37]

As we observe Boiko's reconstructed office, Iryna tells me a story. Seven years ago, an elderly woman from a nearby village visited the museum as part of an organised excursion. The woman had paid visits to Boiko's real office on several occasions in her life with requests for help finding work for her children and paying bills; each time her pleas were heard sympathetically by the benevolent director. On seeing the museum reconstruction, the woman had been overcome with emotion and asked for a photographer to take her picture sitting at the base of the large desk, 'so that her children could know to whom they owed their fate'. Iryna admits that she often tells this story during excursions to illustrate the enterprise's social responsibility and 'love for its people'. Almost on cue, a labourer from one of the steel-rolling workshops walks through the door and hands her a package containing a portrait of Boiko that's been

found on the shop floor. 'We didn't want to throw away such a precious object, so we thought it was better to gift it to the museum,' he explains. Iryna smiles and promises that she will add it to the museum collection.

Before Russia's full-scale invasion of Ukraine, and the military siege that devastated Mariupol and displaced much of its population, worker cults were still going strong in the city. Faced with the brain drain of young people to other more lucrative and less dangerous professions, Rinat Akhmetov's Metinvest company had rebooted the Stakhanovite tradition for the twenty-first century. Aiming to inspire allegiance to the historic enterprise, the final hall of the Ilych Museum is dedicated to 'family dynasties', different generations of the same family who had worked at the factory for an uninterrupted number of years. Mounted portraits of the Kapustnikov family, who had collectively worked 994 years at the plant, and the Rakhuba family, who had completed 480 years of collective labour, are displayed along a ceremonious walkway. Like the original Stakhanovite movement, these symbolic gestures are also backed up by material rewards. As we chat in her office after the excursion, a man knocks on the door and explains that he is there to collect his family-dynasty vouchers. Iryna does some quick calculations on the back on an envelope based on the years his family has worked at the factory. After clarifying some biographical details, she hands over coupons for 2,000 hryvnias (around £40) to be spent in the Ilych factory shop.

In spring 2022, the Ilych Iron and Steelmaking Museum was destroyed by Russian bombing. Fire engulfed the gallery of rooms packed with Soviet-era industrial memorabilia, erasing the difficult heritage had that formed an awkward but fundamental part of modern Ukraine's past. The story of Makar Mazai, the reconstruction of Boiko's office, and the hall of family dynasties were all reduced to ashes. Museum workers tried to save some objects, but the missiles fell too quickly and intensely. It was all that they could do to save themselves by gathering in basements and waiting, for weeks on end in some cases, for the danger to pass. With a tragic irony, Russia succeeded in achieving the decommunisation process in the Ukrainian east that it had so energetically resisted, so vitriolically condemned. The story of Soviet industry in Mariupol, with its tacit celebration of environmental and human exploitation, and its reliance on patriarchal cults, will never be presented the same way again.

Ukraine is gradually doing away with its cults. As Lenin monuments stack up in museum yards and worker-hero myths are erased from the record, a new history is emerging. This history will likely have no space for Soviet industrial romance. It will have no nostalgia for Stakhanovite photography, in which miners clasp bouquets of flowers and welders gaze into the mid-distance, glimpsing communism. And this might be for the best. After all, how can a country move forward towards a modern, post-authoritarian future if it is shackled to the cultural legacies of the Soviet past? How can it craft a new story for itself if its museums are dominated by old myths? But with the erasure of tangible heritage of industry, there is also the erasure of something else, less easy to grasp, that forms part of community identity: a shared sense of belonging to a place where the infrastructure of industry dominates the skyline, and where labour traditions and values have shaped the grammar of everyday life.

FOUR

Bright City

My experience of zabroshka life started in my hometown of Luhansk. Luhansk was, after all, a very rich field site for these kinds of explorations. I started visiting zabroshkas already when I was at school, at that difficult age when you're awkward and full of questions. I saw a zabroshka while I was walking around my neighbourhood and decided to go inside. It was an unfinished, concrete building, a two-floor square block. I went inside and went up to the roof and just looked around, had a think, and listened to music. You know, like everyone does.

I went to school in the district of the first city hospital. It's a really green part of town, the hospital district, in the Hostra Mohyla region. It's a wooded area close to an amazing aircraft unit that was gradually falling into dereliction ... My school was right next to the forest. Later, the aviation school was disbanded and its main administrative corpus – lots of buildings with excellent classrooms – was transferred to our school. My original school stayed in the forest and quickly turned into a zabroshka. Between Classes 3 and 5, I helped transport some things from there, like papers that we collected during our 'volunteer Saturdays', to my new school. I remember seeing lots of documents in the abandoned building and keeping one photograph – a photo of the class of 1963. I still remember the faces of the schoolchildren ... I didn't know that class. I just kept it. And it's only now I realise how much time I spent just looking at the faces of those people, those fixed expressions. The manor house in Luhansk where I used to do ballet classes also turned into a complete zabroshka. I remember the interior decoration of that old building. It was beautiful. And before our very eyes, it decayed into nothing, not even a colonnade was left.

I've always been into all kinds of countercultural things, and my whole being – which I still didn't understand very well back then – was already rebelling and didn't want to witness these kinds of processes. And, of course, I've always taken part in alternative scenes, music and art. And zabroshkas, in this sense, are incredibly atmospheric, spectacular places, where you can stage scenes and take photos. Abandoned places are a kind of matter or architecture stretched out over time. They're something that's always been there, a background to our lives, such a constant that we don't even have to try to articulate it.

The key word here is 'atmosphere'. That is, the ether that connects everything. I got this word from some kids that I met hanging out by a fence near a zabroshka on Gogol Street in Sievierodonetsk. The boys were around ten years old. And I start laughing. And they start laughing, saying 'we've been busted' and all that. And so, I ask them: 'Why is it that you like climbing around these zabroshkas?' And they come back with, 'What do you mean why? For the atmosphere, of course.' And this 'atmosphere' is the key feature that distinguishes zabroshkas from non-zabroshkas, life from non-life, and the dying from the newly born.

Kateryna Syrik
Luhansk, Luhansk region (occupied since 2014)

I AM STANDING awkwardly in the middle of a derelict hangar in Sievierodonetsk's semi-rural edgeland, having arrived several hours too early for a rave. Our Ukrainian colleagues from the city, with whom we're coordinating a two-week summer school for artists working with the region's industrial legacies, have, with some undisguised amusement, invited our 'foreign delegation' to the event to help us understand what life's *really* like in Ukraine's industrial periphery.[1] The rave's been organised by a local activist, who's hired the hangar for pennies from its octogenarian owner and put on an all-star line-up of DJs attracting visitors from across the country. The interior of the hangar is sparsely decorated. A few hard-backed cinema seats scavenged from another derelict building have been transported to the venue for people to sit on and rest between bouts of dancing. Some fairy lights hang from the precarious-looking roof. Against the walls peeling with paint, a light display of shape-shifting geometric shapes is moving to the music. The shapes are interspersed with symbols from the periodic table, a reference to Sievierodonetsk's chemical-making past.

The hangar seems once, not so long ago, to have been part of the sprawling industrial infrastructure that formed the city's massive AZOT chemical-making plant. AZOT, taking its name from the Ukrainian for nitrogen, was one of the most famous chemical producers in the Soviet Union by the 1970s, known from Riga to Vladivostok. Escaping the pounding sound check for a minute, I wander into one of the building's back rooms, a former office by the looks of it, which still contains personal belongings of the people who used to work here. On one wall,

covered with glitzy gold wallpaper, there's a fading Orthodox icon of the Virgin and Child. Below it, forming a somewhat incongruous composition, is a panoramic photo of the AZOT complex, captured with a blurry lens, creating an oddly romantic effect. The office has a small hatch window connecting it with the shop floor, through which the strobe lighting of the rave is flashing. This little room feels like a concentration of history: the past, present and future of the city all melding into one intense and physically experienced moment.

Before it was destroyed and occupied by invading Russian forces, Sievierodonetsk was one of Ukraine's best-preserved mid-Soviet-era monotowns. Monotowns, meaning mono-functional or single-industry urban settlements, didn't exist only in the Soviet Union, but the communist state perhaps came closest to perfecting them. Now associated with derelict industrial infrastructure and suffocating air pollution, monotowns were in their time a manifestation of socialist urban utopianism. It was here that the much-heralded transfiguration of the Soviet person through labour would take place and that a new communist society would finally form. Spending time in Sievierodonetsk in 2019 was therefore to travel back in time to a moment of vanished ideological certainty. To travel back past the outbreak of war in the region that resulted in the city's three-month-long occupation in 2014, past the economic and infrastructural devastation of the freewheeling 1990s, the environmental depletion of the Soviet decades that preceded, to arrive at a moment of unshakeable faith in industrial modernity and its logic of limitless economic growth.

◈

'Sievierodonetsk is a city of chemists.' These are the words with which every self-respecting tour guide will start their excursions, and Oleksandr (Sasha) Kuchynskyi, a quietly spoken local artist who is attending our summer school and doubling up as our host while we're in the city, dutifully rehearses them. I try for a moment to imagine what the British equivalent of 'a city of chemists' might be but can only come up with rough approximations – perhaps Middlesbrough or another town in Teesside? But Sievierodonetsk is a city of chemists in the technical-intelligentsia sense. What's more, here everything revolves round the factory. Thanks to the geometric layout of the city, its iconic silhouette can be seen from almost every street corner. And people's pride in the city's scientific expertise is obvious.

History books from Soviet times like to emphasise that Sievierodonetsk was built on a void. 'Where today there are wide green boulevards and all kinds of industrial objects,' write the historians V. V. Butov and S. A. Pertsovskii, 'for centuries people walked on the desert sands of the desiccated steppe.'[2] This is that romantic idea again of the flourishing of industrial Donbas on barren, empty steppe land, and it isn't one unique to Sievierodonetsk, either. But Sievierodonetsk, before it was Sievierodonetsk and all its factory production lines, was many other things too: as local historians Serhii Kaleniuk and Mykola Lomako explain, the present-day city was at the centre of the Donets borderlands, a region where the interests of the Great Horde and the Crimean Khanate converged, and the meeting point between the Don, Zaporizhzhia, and Sloboda Cossacks.[3] For the production-fixated Soviets, however, this long history was irrelevant. For them, Sievierodonetsk's story begins with the foundation of the chemical works in 1934.

In the airy, plant-filled lobby of Sievierodonetsk's Hotel Central, where we're staying, I study the city on a map. Sievierodonetsk is a prototypical Soviet-era monotown: the huge ammonium-nitrate plant around which the city has been built takes up more than half of the space on the page. Everything else on the map seems just an afterthought to this industrial monolith. The road that divides the manufacturing complex from the residential zone is even named after a former factory director, Bohdan Lishchyna. To the east of Lishchyna Street is a densely populated criss-cross of roads that forms the residential district in which our hotel is located. To the west of this street is the whole spawling world that is the factory complex. This side of town, the private property of the Ukrainian oligarch Dmytro Firtash, is inaccessible to the public without the necessary passes. Today our group of summer-school students is going to the controlled zone to visit the AZOT factory museum.

The story of AZOT's founding, and the formation of Sievierodonetsk around it, is closely intertwined with the story of Stalinist collectivisation and crash industrialisation. Intended to produce the ammonium nitrate for fertiliser that would supersize Soviet agriculture, the factory was first planned for construction in the neighbouring coal-mining town of Lysychansk. When this location turned out to be impractical, planners decided to build the plant on the other side of the Siverskyi Donets river, on a sandy plain that was at that time occupied by a few 'disposable' villages.[4] It was thought at this time that factory workers would live across the river from the factory in a 'Greater Lysychansk', made up of the historic old town plus a brand new socialist city. The steppe climate, however, scuppered these plans: the vulnerability of the low-level bridge to flooding and winter ice drifts meant that, in the end, the new socialist city had to be relocated on the left bank, next to the chemical factory itself.[5] Beginning with a few wooden barracks, the chemists' settlement gradually grew into a fully functioning city: in 1934, Sievierodonetsk was born.

The factory settlement, known only as the Lysychansk Chemical Construction Site ('Lyskhimstroi' for short) until the 1950s, was to be a green and pleasant place, much like the British new towns of Stevenage or Peterlee.[6] The city would comprise a geometric grid of modern high-rise blocks of flats. These blocks would host shops and services on their ground floors, while nurseries, schools, and worker canteens would be built for the communities in each neighbourhood. Between

the high-rise blocks, leafy courtyards would host playgrounds for local children and outdoor gyms in which people could exercise. Cultural life was to be designed into the city: theatres, cinemas, an opera house, clubs, art galleries, and Houses of Culture, would all form part of the urban composition. Soviet architectural critics gushed with enthusiasm for the project: 'Lyskhimstroi will be the clearest proof of the boundless concern our party and its leader, Stalin, have for our people,' the authors of one article effused. 'A socialist city, a bright city – that's what our party and non-party Bolsheviks are building!'[7]

We're walking along the barbed-wire-topped perimeter fence of the industrial zone, looking for the entranceway to the AZOT plant. Today most of the buildings inside seem deserted and Sasha explains that since the war began in 2014, the factory has idled. War damage to the energy grid has made the region dependent on an ageing and damaged local power plant, while the termination of cheap gas from Russia has caused Ukraine's fertiliser industry to stall.[8] On top of this, Sievier's location near the front line of fighting has raised concerns about the risk of a chemical disaster: ammonium nitrate can trigger a massive explosion, much larger than a conventional bomb, if exposed to intense heat, such as a fire resulting from a missile strike.[9] The sharp drop in the factory's activity has resulted in mass unemployment in the chemical city. Neoliberal market forces will have contributed to this decline, but it does remain that before the war, AZOT had employed around 8,000 workers and now that's been reduced to only a few hundred people.[10] One of them is the factory's museum director, Olha Holovka, who is waiting inside the entrance gates to show us around.

The first thing Olha tells us as we enter the museum's grand entry hall is that photography is strictly prohibited. Dmytro Firtash's Oschem company, which controls a group of chemical factories across Ukraine, Estonia, and Tajikistan, is categorical about this, she explains, gesturing to a crossed-through camera sign on the wall. I wonder what industry secrets Firtash is worried will get out. The museum seems to be an uncontroversial Soviet-era exhibit that follows an established narrative arc: oil paintings of a huge construction site romanticise the city's creation by communist youth brigades, while a collection of documentary photography mourns the damage Nazis wreaked on the city a decade later. Further along, worker portraits from the 1960s and 1970s, and a trestle table heaving with chemical-based products (including a brand of PVA glue that I recognise from primary school), testify to the factory's flourishing in the late-socialist era. At the display's centre is a vintage wooden sign embossed with an abstract image of a test tube and a quote from Maxim Gorky: 'Chemistry is the domain of miracles,' it reads, proudly. 'It is here that mankind's happiness is hidden, it is here that great conquests of the mind take place.'

The postwar reconstruction of Sievierodonetsk, also depicted among the museum's exhibits, is a central part of the city's self-mythologisation. With the region's recapture from Nazi occupation in February 1943, and the arrival of industrial equipment looted from eastern Germany, a new phase of chemical production began. According to reports written by communist 'enthusiasts' (the name given to the labour migrants who came, either of their own accord, fired by ideological enthusiasm, or through some coercive mechanism of the Soviet state), people flooded into the region from as far as the Urals and the Far East of Russia, Central Asia and the Caucasus to help with the task of reconstructing the chemical city after the war.[11] Supposed feats of labour, in the form of the improbably quick restoration of buildings and installation of industrial equipment, were recorded daily. By 1948, many factories had been rebuilt, machines put in place, and skilled workers trained. Just three years later, in 1951, the first outputs of light ammonium nitrate (for use in fertilisers) were recorded.[12]

If Gorky's claim that chemistry is the domain of all mankind's happiness seems overblown, Sievierodonetsk, the Soviet city of chemists, does seem like a place where one could be happy. Ukrainians would say that it is *zatyshno* or *uiutno*, in Russian, words that, like *hygge*, evoke an idea of comfort, conviviality. This clearly has something to do with the city's scale: unlike larger ex-socialist metropolises, like Minsk or Warsaw, for example, Sievierodonetsk is entirely walkable, with no unreasonably massive public squares or dangerously busy roads. The geometric planning of the city makes it hard to get lost, while with a bit of practice, you can start finding shortcuts through the patchwork of courtyards that form the shared spaces between blocks of flats. These spaces, which residents have planted out and decorated with their own folk art made from recycled tyres, sculptures, and soft toys, are part of what makes the city feel so warm and welcoming. I realise that, unlike Edinburgh, where I live at the time, I feel entirely safe walking around here at night.

Another striking feature of the city is its greenness. For a place that was apparently built on a desert, life seems to be

bursting forth through every crack in the pavement. But as the writer and journalist Svitlana Oslavska explains, Sievier's greening was partly political. The city was marketed to outsiders as a 'steppe oasis', an urban utopia in which anyone would be lucky to live.[13] This thinking matched the logic of Stakhanovism, which held that labour achievements should be rewarded with the good things in life, from well-stocked shops to well-tended gardens.[14] Far from renouncing these rewards, a good Soviet strike worker would dutifully enjoy the fruits of their labour, engaging in cultured pursuits, from reading in libraries to walking with family members in parks.[15] The steadily rewilding rose patches, flourishing peony and aster borders that line the asphalted streets along which I'm walking are thus the untended legacies of this politicised urban landscaping.

But the greenness of Sievierodonetsk has a sinister side. Built so close to a major ammonium nitrate factory, the city has always had extremely high air pollution levels. The sky-scraping chimneys of the AZOT plant released fine dust and nitric-acid emissions into the air that have been linked in studies to heart and pulmonary diseases.[16] Seeking ways to mitigate these problems, Soviet planners advocated the mass planting of high trees – birches, ashes, and the region's ubiquitous poplars – whose feather-like branches were supposed to comb the sky above of its toxic contents. These trees, which by 2019 have grown to extraordinary heights, sometimes completely obscuring the façades of the buildings in front of which they were planted, are thus toxic-wind breaks, not natural ornaments intended to beautify the city. If greenery was a reward for superhuman feats of labour, it was also a futile attempt to defend against that labour's toxic impact on the health of the local community.[17]

Unlike mining and steelmaking, chemical production was not an easily romanticised industry. The monotonous and largely invisible character of ammonia production made it a difficult subject for celebratory Soviet propaganda films and colourful posters. As the historians Butov and Pertsovskii explain, 'here there is no radiance of incandescent metal as there is for the steelmaker, nor the lustre of curly shavings as there is for the turner'. In their place there was 'the toil of serious, focused technicians, interlacing pipelines and the rhythmical ticking of instruments'.[18] Despite its lack of industrial glamour, however, chemical production still – like all realms of Soviet industry – became an area of intense socialist competition, experimentation and innovation in the second half of the twentieth century. The youthful workforce at AZOT were at the forefront of these processes, throwing their efforts behind the production of chemicals for the acceleration of the Soviet economy and winning high-profile state prizes and accolades in the process.[19]

The first chemists to work at AZOT were labour migrants from Dzerzhinsk and Uzlovaya in south-west Russia, factory towns that had specialised in the production of mustard gas during the 1940s, as well as labourers from the surrounding region. These so-called 'masters' were brought in to train the local workforce in the delicate techniques of ammonia-making. A laborious and inefficient process to begin with, involving the manual operation of pressure gauges and shut-off valves, the production of this chemical was gradually mechanised and refined.[20] By the mid-1970s, local technical colleges were churning out hundreds of graduate chemists, technicians, and mechanical engineers, who joined the growing workforce at the factory. The preponderance of new graduates among

factory employees each year meant that Sievierodonetsk gained the reputation of being a 'city of youth'.[21] Soviet propagandists proudly promoted this fact in a bid to encourage others to move to the city. In political posters and documentary films, young mothers were often depicted pushing prams against the backdrop of the factory's smoking chimney stacks.[22]

Walking back through the centre, our group encounters some architectural indicators of the prestige the city enjoyed before the industry began to decline in the 1980s. On Peace Square, known as Soviet Square until the decommunisation laws of 2015, we arrive in front of the green-and-white colonnaded façade of Sievierodonetsk's Palace of Chemists. The palace is oddly austere by comparison with its neighbours. Dating from the Stalinist 1940s, these buildings include the decorative flourishes, cornicework and marble friezes that the Georgian dictator so admired in classical architecture.[23] The palace's austerity is down to the political conflict that marked the moment of its construction. Begun in 1958, during the height of the Khrushchev 'Thaw', it was caught up in the heated aesthetic debates emerging from de-Stalinisation, when architectural 'extravagances' were critiqued as not in keeping with the anti-imperial values of the Marxist-Leninist regime. The palace, which had been planned to include much more ostentatious decoration, was hastily redesigned at this time as the functionalist-classicist fusion that we now see before us.[24]

Sasha tells us that the palace was restored by Firtash's AZOT company after falling into semi-dereliction in the 1990s. But if it now hosts the occasional concert and festive performance, it plays nothing like the central role in community life that it did in the 1970s. Back then its doors were rarely closed. The palace would have been a busy hub of Soviet labour rituals, hosting celebrations of record-breaking factory collectives, inventors of new chemical processes, and 'labour veterans', as well as rituals initiating young chemists into the Soviet Army.[25] Its neoclassical, high-ceilinged rooms would have been used by professional clubs and political organisations which, at least on paper, were communicating the traditions of Marxist-Leninist thinking to future generations.[26] While these attempts to politically indoctrinate were often met with indifference by the late-Soviet period, the palace no doubt served as a popular youth club for many generations of people growing up in the city.

According to Marxist-Leninist labour theory, a worker's capacity for professional innovation was closely tied to their creativity in other spheres. In other words, to be an experimental, free-thinking chemist or physician, you also had to regularly flex your creative muscles by taking part in song festivals, dance ensembles, landscape painting or photography. The Palace of Chemists provided a space for these creative practices too. According to Butov and Pertsovskii, it was home to more than a dozen self-organised collectives in the 1970s, comprising thousands of local workers. These collectives included a song-and-dance ensemble performing such catchy numbers as 'Chemistry Serves the People' and the all-Soviet classics 'Lenin Road' and 'The Komsomol Youth Has Gone'. Children were encouraged to take part in the creative clubs the palace ran. Folk-song-and-dance ensembles, theatre collectives, and, of course, chemistry clubs were a regular part of after-school life.[27]

It is perhaps the palace's former identity as a hub of local culture, which once made it central to community life, that now makes it feel so culturally peripheral. The large square in front of the building, once used for communist parades and demonstrations, is abandoned when we visit and, despite AZOT's recent renovation and rebranding campaign, a sense of ideological dereliction persists. The circular metal frames that stand in front of the façade and would once have held portraits of the factory's most celebrated workers are now starkly empty. Behind them, untended plants grow slightly higher than they should, creeping into the round frames, suggesting a kind of ideological rewilding. Closer to the centre of the square, where a Lenin monument stood until 2015, there is now an empty plinth mounted with the monumental words 'I ♥ Sievierodonetsk'. Local patriotism has replaced ideological zeal, though this too, according to some, is on somewhat shaky ground.

There is a second palace in Sievierodonetsk. This one is located just outside my hotel, and I decide to walk around it to photograph its beautiful mosaics in the evening once the worst of the afternoon heat has passed. Like the Palace of Chemists, Sievierodonetsk's Ice Palace of Sport has clearly seen better days. Right now it is closed to the public, and despite my cajoling requests, the attendants inside refuse to let me in to look around. There is much to observe from the outside, however. The palace, constructed in the functionalist style that was common for public buildings in the 1970s, is a 'type building', one of a series of identical structures that was built in different regions of the Soviet Union around the same period.[28] A ground floor of paned glass, entryways, and mosaics is crowned by a first level of corrugated iron panelling which forms a gentle arc across the main façade. The structure was designed to house an enormous sports arena that had the capacity to accommodate up to 7,000 people. Aside from similar palaces in Novosibirsk and Riga, it was the biggest stadium of its kind in the USSR when it was built in 1975.[29]

The decision to build an arena of this size in Sievierodonetsk was a nod to the city's strategic importance in the later decades of Soviet rule. During the 1960s and 1970s, the chemical city became a destination of choice for large delegations of industry experts, who would gather there for conferences and exhibitions, to share knowledge and experience and to exchange engineering solutions and new technology. Sievier's local politicians had been lobbying central government for some years to build a prestigious site worthy of hosting these delegations, but, according to Svitlana Oslavska, it was AZOT's connections in Moscow that eventually sealed the deal.[30] Construction began in 1972, with materials and machinery arriving from all over the USSR, and refrigeration equipment even brought in from a company in the German Democratic Republic with which AZOT had been cooperating for many years. The building work was on such a scale that the road leading to the palace became known as the 'ice road', jammed as it constantly was with vehicles transporting huge blocks of ice to the site.[31]

The colourful murals that wrap around the lower floor of the building depict idealised scenes from Soviet sporting and cultural life. On one side, hundreds of tiny tiles in shades of blue, grey, and white form a picture of dancing ice skaters, legs arched in delicate poses, hair flowing in the wind. On the building's opposite side, tiny squares of red and dusky pink combine to create a group of muscular women playing volleyball, the space between them filled by a flock of swooping swallows. Oslavska's deep dive into the history of these murals has revealed that they were the work of various artists, from both Kyiv and Moscow, and were installed as ready-made

bricks transported to Sievierodonetsk from the artists' studios.[32] When the building fell into dereliction in the 1990s, the murals were painstakingly restored by local art historians, who scavenged extra tiles from the palace's basement to patch up the compositions. The efforts of these enthusiasts have not been in vain: with the gradual decomposition of the palace, the bright optimism of the murals is even more striking today.

Above the palace's main entranceway, a bright plastic banner reads 'Congratulations to Our Graduates!' In 2019, the building's vast arena was still host to university graduations and other festive celebrations, but the days of its thousands-strong industrial conferences and international delegations were long gone. At the height of Sievierodonetsk's socialist golden age, when AZOT's youthful workforce was not only winning state awards for its productivity, but also participating in sports competitions, earning the city the reputation of being one of the most athletic in the Soviet Union, the country's biggest rock star played the Ice Palace. Vladimir Vysotsky, the Soviet Union's answer to Bob Dylan, whose gravelly, forty-a-day voice and edgy political lyrics earned him cult status in the late socialist period, packed out the arena in 1978. His visit still lingers in older residents' memories as a marker of a different era, a time when scientific expertise was valued, and the chemical city thrived.

In 2004, a delegation of an entirely different kind had descended on the Ice Palace. Following the Orange Revolution – a series of protests that had disputed the victory of the pro-Russian candidate Viktor Yanukovych at the presidential elections in 2004, and brought Viktor Yushchenko to power – Sievierodonetsk had briefly become the centre of the first so-called 'Russian Spring'.[33] Pro-Russian regional delegates, including Yanukovych himself, the head of the Kharkiv region, Yevhen Kushnarov, and the Mayor of Moscow, Yurii Luzhkov, had all travelled to the city of chemists to debate what they claimed to be an 'anti-state coup'. The vast stadium had been filled with impassioned speeches, some of which had called for the establishment of a 'South-Eastern Autonomous Republic'. Ultimately, Yanukovych had called for caution, warning that the 'orange menace' would only gain strength if blood was spilled. As it turned out, however, Russian efforts to forcibly realise the separatist agenda had already both literally and figuratively been put on ice.

It is easy to understand why, at this time, a limited part of the local community would have been sympathetic to Russian-sponsored separatist ideas. The much-heralded neo-liberal transition after 1991 had failed to deliver its promised economic recovery, instead creating a huge economic gulf in society, enriching a tiny oligarchic elite while impoverishing large swathes of the population.[34] This gulf was felt particularly keenly in monotowns like Sievierodonetsk. Following his purchase of AZOT in 2011, Dmytro Firtash had attempted to ring every *kopiika* from his chemical-making asset. Salaries of workers at the plant were slashed in the early 2010s and conditions worsened in what many believed was a strategic move to run the company into the ground. The plant had begun haemorrhaging employees at this time: contracts fell from 15,000 in 1991, to 11,000 in 2010, to just 7,800 in 2012.[35] Having played a paternalistic role in the city's urban development during Soviet times, bankrolling education, healthcare, and construction, AZOT had started to offload its social responsibilities onto the municipal authorities. Life in the city during these years had become more challenging, with regular power outages, water shortages and cuts to public services.

If Sasha's generation had been too young to recall the first brush with separatism at the Ice Palace, they would certainly remember the next time Russian fighting groups came to the city, ten years later in 2014. Arguing that Donbas had been left to rot by the Ukrainian politicians and that the closures of mines and factories, resulting in whole new districts of dereliction, had been a purposeful policy of targeted disinvestment, Russian propagandists had garnered some limited support in the local community (though most people had kept their heads down). It was at this time that the bridge between Sievierodonetsk and Lysychansk was also bombed for the first time, when the self-proclaimed and unrecognised 'Luhansk People's Republic' fought, with Russian backing, to occupy the region. People and their families had kept out of sight and trouble during the occupation, praying for the quick restoration of peace. It was only when the Ukrainian army liberated the region three months later, pushing the front line of fighting a hundred kilometres down the road, that any kind of normality had resumed.

❖

I am walking with Sasha and some of the summer-school students along Sievierodonetsk's tree-lined Central Prospect, known as Soviet Prospect until 2015. This street is an open-air exhibition of Soviet-era architectural ruins. In addition to the modernist majesty of the Ice Palace and the wing-clipped

austerity of the Palace of Chemists, it also boasts the magnificent socialist-modernist ruin that is Café Mosaic. Approaching this building from a distance, I take in its beautiful proportions – the conical, glass-panelled dining area with a circular flat roof makes it resemble a mid-century UFO. A neat terrace curves around its perimeter, bordered by a green wrought-iron balustrade, where it's easy to imagine people lounging and reading the papers. Mounting the metal steps to the terrace and peering through the ironwork screen and broken glass, I catch a glimpse of a moment frozen in time. The luxurious, full-height cream curtains are pulled back, allowing shafts of light to fall gently into the oval dining space. Despite the dereliction, the place resounds with vintage glamour.

Café Mosaic had in Soviet times been a much-loved local restaurant. When it first opened its doors in 1966, it had been a beer hall, offering drinks and high-end snacks, called Shaiba, meaning Hockey Puck – a reference to its unusual disc-like form. Shaiba had been a popular hangout for factory workers just off their shifts, who could decompress here from a day's chemical manufacturing before returning home.[36] When Gorbachev's prohibition laws were introduced in the mid-1980s, it was forced to reinvent itself as a children's disco and café. Most people's nostalgic memories of the place date from this time and feature childhood experiences of the café's decadent ice-cream sundaes, lurid jellies and lemonades. After socialism, the restaurant was mismanaged by local businessmen, closed, and fell into disrepair. Plans for its renovation in the early 2010s were shelved following the Russian-backed war and occupation of 2014.[37] Frightened off by the threat of renewed military violence, investors abandoned the building to its current state of suspended animation.

A member of our group, Kateryna (Katia) Syrik, who moved to Sievierodonetsk after her hometown of Luhansk was occupied in 2014, explains that there are hundreds of buildings like Café Mosaic in Sievierodonetsk. People call these buildings *zabroshki*, a noun derived from the word *zabroshennyi* in Russian, meaning abandoned, or *zanedbanki* in Ukrainian. When Katia asks how *zabroshka* would be translated into English, we realise that there is no equivalent that renders the ironic affection of the word's diminutive *-shka* ending, also found in *babushka* and *dedushka*, meaning granny and grampy.[38] Abandoned buildings, ruins, brownfield sites . . . all these terms seem somehow too formal, too administrative. The gap in the vocabulary is indicative of a gap in the cultural reality. There is nothing like the extent of architectural dereliction in the UK that there is in Donbas, despite the UK's UrbEx movement being a touchstone for many of those in Ukraine who like to explore abandoned buildings.[39] The combined

E. P. Kovalevskyi's 'Petrographic map of the Donets Mountainous Ridge . . . created on the basis of observations and discoveries between 1823 and 1827'. Reproduced with permission of the Vernadskyi National Library of Ukraine in Kyiv.

Ruins of the 'Bakhmutska sil' salt mine complex in Pidgorodne village near Bakhmut. 2021. Photo: Mykhailo Kulishov.

Yard decorations in Sievierodonetsk. 2019.

*Hollyhocks in central Sievierodonetsk. 2019. Photo: Oliver McKenzie;
tyre planter in Pokrovsk. 2021; steppe grasses at the Regional
Landscape Park 'Kleban-Byk' near Kostiantynivka. 2021.*

Bilokuzmynivka Chalk Cliffs, Bilokuzmynivka Village. 2021.

A sink hole in Striapivka gypsum mine near Soledar. 2021.

Chalk slag heaps and steppe flowers near Sloviansk. 2021.

A cave in Bilokuzmynivka Chalk Cliffs, Bilokuzmynivka Village. 2021.

A tunnel inside Salt Mine No. 1 in Soledar. 2021.

An excursion across the steppe near Soledar. 2021.

A walk across the salt marshes near Striapivka. 2021.

A guided tour of the Kramatorsk Machine Building Factory. 2021.

Visiting the 'Central' Mine in the frontline city of Toretsk. 2021.

'Restaurant with all the bells and whistles'. Our Little Nook Café, Mariupol. 2021.

Purple metal spirals at the Kramatorsk Machine Building Factory. 2021.

Smoke rising from a factory in Mariupol. 2021.
Photo: Artem Bereznev.

Wine stored in a former gypsum mine at the Artwinery cellars
in Bakhmut. 2021.

Marsh samphire growing on the salt marshes near Kostianynivka. 2021.

Sink hole in the Striapivka gypsum mine near Soledar. 2021.
Photo: Mykhailo Kulishov.

Pink skies over Mariupol. 2021. Photo: Artem Bereznev.

Raihorodok chalk deposit, Raihorodok Village. 2021.

Interior of Café Mosaic in Sievierodonetsk. 2019.

Advert for Crimean sparkling wine at Artwinery cellars in Bakhmut. 2021.

Mosaic of skiers on the Ice Palace in Sievierodonetsk. 2019.

Seagulls fly over the Azov Sea in Mariupol. 2021.

violence of unbridled neoliberal market economics and, since 2014, neo-imperial Russian warfare has left a deep imprint on the region, turning productive and peopled industrial districts into empty ghost towns.

Katia and Sasha form part of a community of young people that goes exploring *zabroshki* in their spare time. On foot or by car, they venture to the region's dilapidated Soviet warehouses and factory buildings, scavenging objects and papers that, as Katia explains, have been discarded as 'historical trash'. When I ask what the attraction of visiting these places is for the group, Katia answers in mystical terms that time 'smoulders' in *zabroshki*, that matter transforms there before your very eyes: ceilings hang a little lower and walls crack a little further each time you visit. Sasha adds that since he started visiting *zabroshki*, he has been able to better understand the difficult fate of Donbas. Piecing together the discarded fragments of the region's Soviet past, he has been able to establish a more complete picture of the processes of industrial decline and infrastructural collapse that resulted from the imposition of the free market in the 1990s.[40]

Sasha and Katia's group are curating the artefacts that they collect from local *zabroshki* into an 'Archive of De-Industrialisation'. Back at Shakhmatnoe, a former Soviet chess club turned DIY community arts space that is hosting our summer school, they invite us to take a look around their collection. In one of the building's back rooms, painted in bright yellow Soviet-era emulsion, there are tables piled high with reels of undeveloped film, stacks of black-and-white photographs, sepia journals filled with spidery writing, amateur oil paintings, clocks, bottles, and gas masks. The group isn't precious about preserving these objects in a museum-like state, however. Some have been incorporated into art installations. One of these bricolages, a bust of Tchaikovsky daubed with paint and love hearts, and surrounded by garden ornaments, dog toys, and cutlery, stands in Shakhmatnoe's dimly lit entrance hall. Other objects have been repaired or creatively upcycled. Sasha shows me an antique-looking wall light that he has made using coloured filters he found in an abandoned glass factory: the light shining through the green-and-yellow glass casts fairy-like shadows that dance around the room.

The guerrilla preservation work being carried out in Sievierodonetsk reminds me of grassroots projects in South Wales to preserve the region's industrial history. When I was growing up in the 1980s, this heritage was also considered

'trash', the embarrassing relic of a politically compromised past that was better cleared away from view with European Union money. Walking around the Valleys today, you'd be forgiven for not realising that this was, just decades ago, a centre of heavy industry. Where there were once sprawling factory complexes like AZOT, there are now industrial estates and shopping centres. The material traces of the region's industries are today mostly preserved by ex-miners and steelworkers in a network of underfunded, volunteer-run museums. Like Sasha and Katia, these enthusiasts have taken it upon themselves to gather together the pieces of this fragmented history, preserving for future generations a record of their region's complex industrial past.

On the last day of our visit, we take a trip to another well-loved local *zabroshka*. The building is a so-called 'long-build' (*dovhobud*), one of the many construction projects abandoned in the 2000s due to bankruptcy or corruption, which had once been intended to house an IT hub and training centre for students and young specialists from AZOT and other industrial plants. Our group has agreed to meet on the roof of the building site to drink beer and take in the sunset. Crossing the building's threshold through a hole cut in the chain-link fence, we follow a makeshift path through the rubble that suggests the frequency of visitors to the site. We climb a set of concrete stairs that has come away from the wall and looks worryingly precarious, passing floors of heavily graffitied rooms that are clearly well-used hangouts of local teenagers. On the roof the most remarkable view awaits us. Bathed in late-evening sunlight, the urban landscape of concrete high-rises ends abruptly, giving way to rolling, forested steppe. Here, more than anywhere else in the city, one feels the utopian hubris of Soviet industrial modernity: Sievierodonetsk, the Soviet city of chemists, feels somehow stranded here, deep in post-Soviet Ukrainian steppe.

That night, as we sip our beers and watch the ebbing sunlight, I ask Sasha what he would like to see done with the region's many abandoned industrial buildings. Would he prefer them to be reanimated as part of a reindustrialised and economically thriving Donbas, or dismantled and cleared from sight like the former steelworks of South Wales? He tells me that his dream would be for them to be adapted into community centres or arts spaces, places where artists and activists like those who gather at Shakhmatnoe could continue to conduct their work. He talks about the derelict Belgian-built caustic-soda factory in Lysychansk: couldn't this become a community hub filled with co-working spaces, plants, and smiling young creatives like those you see in Warsaw or Berlin? But these dreams have no chance of being realised while war's still raging on just hours away down the road. Who in their right mind, he asks, would invest in the region's derelict industrial infrastructure when it might any day be razed to the ground by an off-course Russian missile?

Sasha had been more prescient than I had realised that night. The Belgian-built industrial relics in Lysychansk, which had hosted all-night raves and dynamic activist festivals, attracting audiences from across Ukraine, were destroyed by Russian bombs in 2022. He sent me photos of the handsome, red-brick buildings in flames from the basement he was sheltering in, followed by images of Lysychansk's half-derelict oil refinery, which burnt for three days, turning the sky black with huge plumes of dirty smoke, and the nitric-acid plant in neighbouring Rubizhne, which, following hits by Russian bombs, sent mushroom clouds of toxic orange gases into the atmosphere. Sievierodonetsk was razed to the ground by Russian shelling, which hit the city repeatedly throughout the summer of 2022. The Ice Palace of Sport burnt down following a missile strike, its mosaics horribly charred. The activist community and their preservationist projects were pushed out of the city. Today, under Russian occupation, its history is being twisted in a different direction.

FIVE

Pink Skies

The last time I built a biotope – an aquarium reconstruction – was in my native Mariupol, together with a young helper, Daniil. We were assembling one of our local reservoir, the Kalchyk River, for our entry to the Ukrainian Competition of Young Biotopists.

Now I stand on the banks of a new mountain river, which I know only as a fisherman who used to come to this place in autumn, when you can see the most striking kinds of endangered plants flowering here. I look around. I make out an unusual sound – the crackle of wet snow falling on electricity lines. I try to put this out of my mind and listen instead to the river. The River Prut is calm in January, but its current is strong and it's noisy. It presses me down into my waders, trying to tip me over and touch my hair with its icy fingers.

I turn over a couple of rocks near the shore. There's nothing under them but the dead remains of some algae. Going in up to my knees in the coastal current, I turn over a different rock and find a mayfly tucked underneath it. She's very surprised and, from inside the last droplet of water on the rock, looks at me with her two large eyes, her triple tail resting beautifully on the stone. Aha, I think – the first water creature for my aquarium installation.

I release the mayfly into a small container and take a couple of photos – I need to look at them back at home in more detail to determine what kind of scene it will make. 'At home' – I always try to find a substitute for these words, remembering the place where I've spent every night for the past year. The phrase 'let's go back' also has a destructive effect on my thoughts – it's become more and more unclear and incomprehensible what that means with each passing day away from home, from the Azov Sea, from the steppe.

Out of the corner of my eye, I register some movement. I find myself back at the water's edge; the movement is somewhere in the treetops – it's a green woodpecker flying overhead. It seems almost as if he's not flying at all, as if it's not flight, but rather a slow fall – two flapping wings and a prolonged dive. The woodpecker flies to a safe landing spot. I breathe out, relieved that he's alive and can continue his explorations of this frosty beauty.

Artem Bereznev

Mariupol, Donetsk region (occupied since 2022)

I FIRST VISITED the southern port city of Mariupol in winter 2021 when Russian troops were building ominously at the border. I arrived early on a morning streaked with straggly grey clouds and, stepping off the overnight train, immediately encountered the stench of metal-making. Metallurgy might not be a smell that many in the now mostly post-industrial UK are familiar with today, unless of course you live in Port Talbot or Scunthorpe. But not that long ago it would have permeated the Valleys of South Wales and cities of North Lanarkshire. Until the 1980s the sprawling Ebbw Vale steel mill, near my home in Cardiff, was one of the biggest in Europe. Like Metinvest, the holding company in Mariupol, its tentacles reached into many areas of local life, including my own. When I was growing up, my dad was employed as a salesman of industrial packaging for steel. He kept cardboard samples of the rolls in his office at our home, where I'd make them into rows of houses for my dolls.

Metallurgy has a range of smells, depending on what process is taking place. The smell I encounter stepping off the train in 2021 is a more pungent version of Fireworks Night: a rotten-egg whiff of naphthalene in coking ovens. People living in Mariupol were familiar with this smell, which rolled regularly through their city like a noxious blanket being spread over a bed. People knew to take their washing in when this smell arrived and, if they were hypervigilant, to call their children in from playing outside. It was the particles of dust that accompanied this smell that caked the windows of their high-rise flats, causing owners to hang out of them, cleaning panes that had been washed only a week before. It was this smell that in 2018 reached such suffocating levels that groups of activists began to protest by wearing gas masks in the streets and on public transport. It was this smell that suddenly disappeared when the city was reduced to ruins by Russian forces in 2022.

A friend in Mariupol once compared the city to Gary in Indiana, which is also home to an enormous steelworks. But while Gary has just one metallurgy complex in which four blast furnaces dirtily smelt iron ore into molten metal, Mariupol had two – Azovstal and Ilych, which hosted six and five blast furnaces each, respectively. What's more, while Gary and other metallurgy cities in the US are subject to strict controls and their owners forced to invest in expensive filtering technology, Mariupol's industries, managed by the Donetsk-born oligarch Rinat Akhmetov, lagged far behind. Particularly galling for local people was the fact that Metinvest's other factories, located in more well-regulated EU countries, were

known to be less polluting than their Ukrainian counterpart.[1] Despite being from the east of Ukraine himself, Akhmetov had no pity, it seemed, for the workers and residents who lived and prematurely died in close proximity of his fortune-generating industrial asset.

When Mariupol's two steelmaking enterprises were being built with foreign investment in the 1890s, they were assigned the poetic-sounding names of Providence and Nikopol. Providence, with its association of spiritual protection against harm, might seem like a symbolic nod to the challenges of life in this over-industrialised city, as if only God could help local people and ecologies to thrive. But the materials that foreign enterprises produced to advertise their steelmaking companies showed no evidence of coded environmental concern. The blast furnaces that would gradually suffocate the local population were in fact a favourite subject of corporate photography.

These furnaces were often pictured from below, ascending like Gothic cathedrals towards the heavens. Rather than being symbols of slow violence and environmental destruction, they were the secular icons of the industrial age.[2]

The nationalisation of industry after 1917 and the frenzied celebration of industrial modernity under Stalin meant there was little space for ecological criticism in early Soviet life.[3] In a state that prioritised industrial production above all else, a smoking chimney stack was a categorically positive image: a sign that work was underway, people were employed, cities were being built, and culture was developing. Criticisms of industry were therefore limited to state-sanctioned topics such as urban planning and filtering technologies.[4] Any more serious critiques could draw accusations of being a 'wrecker' (*vreditel'*, an official term for those accused of purposely inflicting harm on Soviet infrastructural projects), 'hooligan', 'traitor', or 'saboteur'. If you thought you resented working near a roaring blast furnace, worse fates could certainly be found. You might end up part of the enslaved labour force in one of eastern Magadan's deadly gold mines or working in northern Vorkuta's freezing timber industry, where the sun rose just an inch above the horizon in winter.

It would take an ecological disaster on a scale that would shake the world before industry's environmental impact began to be discussed in mainstream Soviet media. The explosion of the No. 4 reactor at the Chornobyl nuclear power plant in April 1986 radically changed what was and wasn't possible to criticise about Soviet industry, even if politicians did everything in their power to cover it up.[5] It was at this time that the term 'ecocide' first began to be used by Ukrainian environmental groups to refer to the incremental damage caused to environments and communities by unlimited industrial growth.[6] In Mariupol, 900 kilometres south of Chornobyl, these questions were explored in amateur filmmaking and photography circles that formed around the studios housed in the city's steelmaking factories. Rather than producing images and film solely for the purposes of propagandising industrial production, factory workers began to document the air and water pollution that they could see taking place around them.[7]

Where Are We Going?, a documentary film from 1989, captures the new spirit of openness around questions of environmental damage and destruction.[8] Housed in the archives of the Mariupol Local History Museum, the film documents growing environmental consciousness in the region during the perestroika era.[9] Beginning with establishing shots of the city's metallurgy works, set to a romantic soundtrack of orchestral strings, the film quickly changes gear to deliver a list of shocking statistics, from the levels of air pollution (thirty times higher than Simferopol in Crimea) to congenital illnesses among children (ten times higher than in central Soviet republics, including those where nuclear weapons were tested). Following this disturbing information, the film's narrator addresses the viewer directly, entreating them to self-organise and challenge the toxic status quo. People are instructed to advocate for the installation of new air-cleaning technology and for an end to the industrial pollution of the Azov Sea. Triggered by the devastating consequences of the Chornobyl catastrophe and enabled by the shifting parameters of public debate about pollution, *Where Are We Going?* was a turning point for ecological activism in the city.

Chornobyl became a touchstone for environmental activism in Mariupol. On the fourth anniversary of the disaster in 1990, protesters gathered outside the Azovstal works, blocking traffic and holding signs bearing such slogans as 'Down with administrations that sacrifice the health of young people for the sake of the Plan'. Protests such as these were documented by local photographers. In Borys Dembytskyi's black-and-white images, which were published in the weekly *Priazovskyi Worker* newspaper, citizens are pictured holding placards and signing petitions, demanding improvements to air-purification technology and expertise.[10] These pictures document the rise of ecological awareness in Mariupol, but also people's growing intolerance for a deceitful political system that sacrificed the health of its citizens for economic gain. Just a year after Dembytskyi took these photos, the USSR itself would collapse, along with the state's sponsorship of the military industrial complex. Mariupol's steel industries would enter a wild and unregulated neoliberal market economy.

Walking through central Mariupol one evening, I was taken aback by the neon-orange sunset that underlit the purplish clouds above, creating a slightly ominous effect. Natives of the Donetsk region will tell you about this psychedelic phenomenon. Some put it down to the steppe's iconic flatness and broad, open skies. Others explain it in more sinister terms, as a chemical reaction caused by industrial toxins in the atmosphere. Nearly everyone that evening was photographing the sunset, while children tore about on the square shouting, and a man sold helium-filled balloons while playing disco tunes from a battered old amp. Looking back at my photos from Scotland half a year later, I realised that I had been standing on Theatre Square. In spring 2022, the theatre there in which citizens and children were sheltering was bombed: 600 of the 1,000 people hiding, terrified, were killed. I remember stopping that night to study the theatre's decorative frieze, which featured a steelworker flanked by representatives of the arts, musicians playing folk instruments gazing towards him with reverence. The frieze remained eerily intact after the bombing; the image I found of it online showed it standing like a Roman ruin. Behind the frieze was only blank open sky.

The square in front of the theatre will now for ever be associated with the word *DETI*, meaning CHILDREN, which was graffitied on the ground in huge letters in a futile attempt to discourage Russian soldiers from directing their missiles at the site. Before 2022, however, it was known for another reason. It was here, in 2018, that huge crowds gathered to protest the city's appalling air quality and chant the words of the viral hashtag *khochu dishat'* (I want to breathe) during the Mariupol Day of the Town celebrations. In the YouTube footage from these protests, figures dressed in white boiler suits and gas masks stand facing the crowd.[11] Above the audience's chatter, a recorded voice can be heard delivering stark facts about Metinvest's poisoning of the city's air. The voice is interspersed with recorded footage of mealy-mouthed pensioners thanking Rinat Akhmetov in effusive Soviet style for all he's done for Mariupol. The camera pans round to show hundreds of people in facemasks. Now a familiar scene, this was a whole year before the Covid-19 pandemic had even begun.

It's difficult to find accurate statistics on levels of air pollution in Mariupol. According to the local activist and opposition politician Maksym Borodin, Metinvest had the local government in its pocket and controlled the timing and conditions of the air-monitoring tests, making this data unreliable.[12] Some things are known, however. According to one local organisation, recorded levels of PM2.5 (tiny dust particles that, once breathed in, enter the bloodstream, concentrating in organs and causing disease) in the city were fifty times the World Health Organization's recommended maximum.[13] In 2006 epidemiologists also discovered extraordinarily high levels of exposure to polycyclic aromatic hydrocarbons (PAHs), linked to lung and skin cancer, among three-year-old children living close to the Azovstal and Ilych plants.[14] Anecdotally, many who grew up in the city suffered from asthma and other chronic respiratory problems, and people often complained of migraines.

Breathing in Mariupol's contaminated air, you breathed in the history of entangled colonialisms in this region of Europe, the Russian imperial politics that invited foreign investment in its newly colonised periphery, and the capitalist competition that led to two huge steel mills being founded here in the 1900s.

Taking another breath, you breathed in the slow violence of Soviet industrialisation that prioritised hyper-productivity far above human life and made a secular religion of industrial modernity, substituting cathedral spires with chimney stacks. Those particles that descended to your lungs were part of the most recent chapter in this history that saw market transition turn to market theft and made billionaires of business-savvy swindlers. The air there was charged with a neoliberal logic that prioritised profit over air-filtering technologies that could have spared the local community's health. The request was simple, yet confronted a whole world of political violence: 'I want to breathe.'

I meet Artem at his aquarium store on a bustling shopping street in central Mariupol. A friend has told me that he is a pillar of the local environmentalist community and will be able to tell me more about the industry-related ecological

issues that the city is currently facing. He is chatting to a customer about the latest filtration equipment when I arrive, and
gestures to me that he won't be long. While I wait, I wander
around his exhibition of fish tanks. Artem makes biotopes,
replicas of underwater habitats from around the world, which
he enters into international competitions. These habitats are
works of great skill that involve sourcing difficult-to-find,
regionally specific plants and creatures that are then assem-
bled into curated scenes. The aquariums on display include
perfect reproductions of the rocky bottom of Lake Malawi
in Tanzania, populated by brightly coloured cichlids, and
the shell-lined base of Lake Tanganyika at Zongwe in the
Democratic Republic of the Congo. Alongside these exotic
underwater seascapes is an aquatic habitat closer to home: the
sandy ridges of the Kalchyk River that flows around the northern outskirts of Mariupol's hyper-polluting Azovstal plant.

Artem finishes with his customer and begins to tell me
about his work. Like many Mariupol men, he at first presents like
an off-duty soldier: the closely cropped hair, camouflage jacket
and serious expression suggesting military training and disci-
pline. As I express my enthusiasm for his curated aquariums,
however, his expression and stance change and I get a totally different impression of him. Artem is clearly a specialist who has
learned his trade first-hand, up to his knees in local rivers and
estuaries, but he is also disarmingly, endearingly funny, talking
passionately about his love of fishing, which he inherited from
his grandfather, who, like him, fished in his spare time when
he wasn't working at the steelworks. I can understand how he's
become a cult figure in the local community. His single-minded
passion is infectious and he can't wait to share his knowledge.

In recent years Artem has been successful in applying for small grants to support his biotope-building project and now has a club of fish enthusiasts who gather regularly at his shop. He mentors young people interested in marine biology and supports them to make replica habitats of their own. Many of the enthusiasts in his community are fishermen themselves, he explains, and so the club doubles up as a discussion forum for exchanging information about water pollution and local ecosystems. In a city where this kind of information is strictly controlled, this fishing club is one of the most expert committees able to determine the damage being wreaked to Mariupol's environmental landscape. Artem tells me that he is preparing a larger grant application to support his work testing and monitoring the city's water quality. These plans, however, will never come to fruition in Mariupol, as the Russian invasion will displace Artem and his community of activists just months later.

Artem has an additional hobby that competes for his time: photography. He suggests that we meet later that same evening to drive around the city and visit some of his favourite industrial spots in Mariupol to photograph. Alongside his biotope-building club, he's part of an amateur photography collective that meets monthly to view slide shows of each other's work and cheerfully criticise each other's photography techniques. For Artem, who has for several decades worked at the Ilych factory, in recent years as a workshop manager, the metallurgy plants are a favourite theme. He particularly likes to photograph the factories at night, when the electric reds and oranges from the furnaces make them look their most dramatic. 'If you catch it at the right time, when the sun is setting behind them and the reds spread out against the sky, it's almost unbearably postapocalyptic,' he says, chuckling.

Later that night, we drive to a distant spot on the bank of the river Kalchyk from where you get one of the best views of Azovstal. Artem parks the car and points out a vaguely trampled track for me to follow, through brown, brittle reeds. I begin to walk into the darkness, guided only by the light of the factory on the other side of the river. I experience a brief sense of panic as I imagine myself lost in this confusing marshland, before Artem catches up and sets me back on the right path. After walking into the pitch black for some minutes, we exit the reedy maze and find Artem's fishing shack, facing the factory. The contrast between the pastoral setting of this rickety wooden hut, fitted with handmade benches for fishermen, and the awesome might of Azovstal across the water is staggering. So close to the factory, the air is filled with the sound of clanging metal and the oceanic roar of the blast furnaces, intermixed with calls of night-time birds and splashing.

Artem tells me that Azovstal has never stopped working. If the furnaces were to idle, they would quickly harden into a huge mass of solid iron that would be impossible to restore, he says. Even during World War II and then in 2014, when the city was briefly occupied by Russian military and Russian-backed

fighting groups, the blast furnaces continued to operate. It would take Russia's months-long siege in spring 2022, when bombs rained down on the city seemingly without end, to finally extinguish their eternal flames. Before we leave the shack, Artem hands me a fishing float that he's found underneath the bench. The red bauble fed through with twisted chicken wire makes me imagine the fishermen who come here to pursue their favourite hobby. Back in Scotland, thinking back to that night-time expedition, I hold this float in my hand and wonder how many of those fishermen are still there now, in occupied Mariupol. What do they think about as they look across the river at the now ruined steel mill that once dominated their city?

Artem has one more thing he wants me to see before we leave. We hop back into the car and drive down the deserted highway to arrive outside Azovstal steelworks. Just outside the factory's monumental entranceway, where cars and buses are pulling in to take people home after their shifts, a group of men in waterproofs and waders is fishing in the scum-topped river. The group's fishing seems to be in flagrant contempt for factory rules. A sign at the end of a set of metal steps leading down to the water reads, 'Swimming and fishing is prohibited. Water outlet No.4.' I ask Artem what's going on, and he explains that the warm wastewater used in the factory's cooling processes is ejected into the river here, bringing shoals of fish to the shore. Despite knowing that the water contains concentrations of contaminants like heavy metals and phenol, the off-duty workers can't resist the easy catch.

Fishing in a contaminated river might at first seem like an act of wilful self-harm. But it might also be understood as part of resourceful practices of 'toxic commoning', as described by anthropologist of waste Patrick O'Hare. [15] Commoning is normally understood as the establishment of alternative public spaces and social relations outside of the market economy. In Ukraine, it is personified by the pensioners who sit outside metro stations selling foraged mushrooms and berries in plastic buckets to passers-by. The twist in heavily polluted cities like Mariupol is that this kind of commoning takes place in a toxified landscape where industrialisation has created new, often hazardous urban environments. Over time, people have found ways to derive economic and social benefit from these places, from a free dinner to a free venue for a rave. Living with pollution and its social consequences was part of what it meant to be from Mariupol before its occupation. Now, as a result of Russia's military assault, the city is dealing with new – material and ideological – kinds of toxic waste.

The bus to the Left Bank, Mariupol's historic working-class district, is packed. We're still in the middle of the pandemic, but it seems like it's only me, the fussy foreigner, who is taking any precautions. Squashed at the front of the bus, the rain lashing down and the windscreen wipers working furiously, I stare at a TV monitor running on a loop. Between commercials for small businesses, there is a more unexpected announcement. Nineteen-year-old Bohdan, dressed in navy cadet uniform, is speaking about recent developments in the city beneath a red-and-blue United States Agency for International Development (USAID) logo. At the bottom of the screen, an English-language rolling banner reads: 'This important initiative helps people meet their own needs in the city.' I'm a bit confused by the video, which seems to be intended for English-speaking audiences, rather than my fellow passengers, most of whom are paying no attention. I decide to look up the programme that Bohdan is advertising when I get back to my hotel that night.

Democratic Governance East turns out to be a contract for over $57 million that began in February 2019 and was intended to run until September 2023. This was part of the US government's initiative to support democracy-building in eastern Europe; investment in the Ukrainian east intensified following the Russian-backed occupation of parts of the Donbas region. Mariupol's perceived vulnerability to Russian military violence after its occupation in May 2014 had prompted USAID to invest heavily in the region. The presence of this funding could be felt across the city: from the historic red-brick water tower in the centre, which had been converted into a creative workspace and exhibition venue, to much smaller-scale initiatives like Artem's environmentalist projects teaching young people about local waterways and raising awareness of pollution caused by heavy industry.

Our bus pulls in at a stop next to a large children's park where I've arranged to meet the Mariupol filmmaker and founder of the Freefilmers collective, Sashko Protyah. Sashko makes socially engaged, independent films about local communities in the Ukrainian east that challenge stereotypical imaginings of the region as a place of post-industrial dereliction and decay.[16] Several of Sashko's films take place in the Left Bank, where he works collaboratively with residents to make textured social portraits of the area. This work stands out against a landscape of filmmaking about Donbas that has tended to exoticise the region as a place to be celebrated (in Soviet propaganda), demonised (in the hyper-bleak portraits of the 1990s), or feared (in the media coverage that followed the occupation in 2014).[17] I've been following and teaching his work for several years, so I'm excited to meet him at last.

Sashko arrives through the rain, his hoodie tight around his face, to where I'm sheltering under a bandstand, and immediately begins to deconstruct the urban scene in front of us. He talks quickly in effortlessly fluent English, which comes from years teaching and translating for visiting foreigners, and giggles often at his own mischievous jokes. The park we are in, he tells me, was recently renovated with USAID money, which paid for the shiny new paving stones, space-age children's attractions, and coiling lampposts that look like they might reference the steelmaker's iconic rodding stick. 'This development was a huge deal for the local community,' Sashko explains. 'The Left Bank used to be one of the most deprived, underfunded regions of the city.' Constructed in the 1930s on the ruins of the Cossack farms and villages that were destroyed after the Bolshevik Revolution, it was originally a settlement of barracks-style houses for the builders and, later, workers at the Azovstal metallurgy plant. Factory workers continued to live in the district throughout the Soviet period. While its identity changed after socialism, with more young people moving in due to the low rents, it still retained something of its former reputation.

After the events of 2014, the district became infamous as the location of the headquarters of the Azov Battalion, a paramilitary group with ultranationalist elements that was incorporated into the National Guard of Ukraine in 2015. During the siege of the city in 2022, Azov fought fiercely to resist the Russian invaders and around 700 of their soldiers were taken prisoner. Azov subsequently became military shorthand for patriotic self-sacrifice during the war, and images of regiment members with the tagline 'Free Azov!' were plastered over billboards all across the country. As we pass Azov's headquarters in 2021, a stonewalled complex housed in a former orphanage and encircled by barbed wire, Sashko asks if I can tell the plainclothes soldiers from civilians. You have to pay attention to the haircut, as well as the fashion sense, he says, to play this game.

One of Russia's false justifications for its invasion in 2022 was that Ukraine had been hijacked by neo-Nazis and was on the brink of ethnically cleansing its Russian population.[18] This claim derived its credibility for audiences in Russia from the Soviet-era myths about World War II, which emphasised the atrocities committed by the Ukrainian Insurgent Army (the UPA) against Ukrainian Jews and Poles, at the same time as it fought for Ukraine's independence. Putin has weaponised this history to argue that neo-Nazis continue to dominate Ukrainian politics, pointing to the political presence of representatives of Pravyi Sektor and Svoboda, groups that took inspiration from the ideology of interwar Ukrainian nationalism and the UPA's struggle for national liberation.[19] When in February 2022, to Putin's surprise, Russian speakers in the east showed intense loyalty to Ukraine, resisting their unwanted 'liberation' by the Russian military, the government explained this away as Nazi brainwashing, calling ominously for a thorough 'de-Nazification' of Ukrainian society, which many interpreted as a call for genocide.[20]

In Russia's warped version of the war, the Azov Battalion in Mariupol were the symbolic representatives of Ukraine's neo-Nazi turn after 2014. Formed in the aftermath of Russia's military operation, the paramilitary organisation did recruit some far-right elements who reportedly made use of neo-Nazi symbols, such as the swastika and SS bolts. After fighting in parallel with the Ukrainian army, Azov was incorporated into the Ukrainian National Guard, a military force with the function of maintaining public order, under the command of the Ministry of Interior.[21] While Azov always retained some ultraconservative elements, these formed a minority within the broader context of the Ukrainian military and were not representative of the views of the Ukrainian public. Even in Mariupol, where one might have expected Azov to retain some popularity with the local community, people were unenthusiastic about their presence. As Sashko explains, with the renovation of the Left Bank, the district has become an attractive, even desirable area for young families, who can be seen walking with prams along the park's newly paved paths. For these new residents, the presence of an armed military unit in their midst is an unwelcome reminder of past times, a political blot on the quickly gentrifying local landscape.

Sashko leads us through the Left Bank district down to the shore of the Azov Sea. I've wanted to see this geographical wonder for years and, despite the foul weather today, am delighted when the brown and choppy waters creep into view over the horizon. The Azov Sea is what's called an inland shelf sea that is connected to the much larger Black Sea to the south by the Strait of Kerch. It is fed by the Don and the Kuban, rivers which deposit sand, salt, and shells at its base, causing the coastline around it to fracture into jagged spits and estuaries. The sea is famously shallow. Soviet tourist photographs of Mariupol show bathers far out in the waters and still only submerged up to their knees. The rivers' flow into the sea means that the water has low salinity and high biomass, making green algae thrive. These unique conditions make for interesting swimming. Friends tell me that at some times of year the sea is covered by frothy, fizzing foam and almost seems to be alive as you move through it.

The plentiful plankton in the Azov Sea means that there has always been abundant wildlife here. At the Mariupol Local History Museum, destroyed by fire after a Russian missile strike in 2022, there was a diorama composed of the many species of bird that dwelt in these shallow waters: shovelers, pintails, and bitterns, white and grey herons, red-necked grebes and common teals all made up part of the stylised, taxidermied display. The sea's shallows were also once rich with fish. Silvery vimba bream, slimline Caspian shemaya, and prehistoric-looking sturgeon all crowded its waters. Several varieties of dolphin, short-beaked and bottlenosed, would also once have visited regularly from the Black Sea. One kind of snub-nosed harbour porpoise, which would migrate here during the summer reproductive season, was once so common that it came to be known as the *Azovka* or Azov dolphin. Between 2001 and 2013, overfishing of these waters caused the dolphin's numbers to drop by 60 per cent.[22] Numbers never recovered. The military conflict in the neighbouring territories, which brought mines and other kinds of military waste to these placid waters, made them increasingly inhospitable for all kinds of marine life after 2014.

The concrete steps down which we've descended the steep hillside suddenly give out onto a beachside restaurant called Nash kutochok, 'Our Little Nook'. The wind is howling now, making it difficult to imagine this place in summer, but it has clearly been a well-loved local spot over the years. Out front there are a selection of Soviet-era attractions, a

face-through-the-hole photograph board of an ice skater in Ukrainian folk dress, and a helter-skelter waterslide that has clearly seen better days. Sashko points to a mechanical sign advertising the restaurant. A glamorous woman in a 'Marilyn Monroe on the subway grate' pose holds a metal sign overhead bearing the words *Restoran s pribambasami*. Sashko translates the sign in his playful English as 'restaurant with all the bells and whistles'. 'There are some things from the Soviet past that you'd still like to hang on to,' he says, with a smile.

The Soviet legacy here is far from all playful kitsch. The collapse of the Azov Sea's delicate ecosystem is mostly the fault of the Soviets, who thought they could harness nature's powers to serve the purposes of their Five Year Plans. The construction of hydroelectric stations upstream and the redirection of rivers for irrigation systems resulted in a 30 to 40 per cent drop in the volume of water entering the sea in the second half of the twentieth century.[23] The knock-on effects of this withdrawal have been extreme. With less fresh water entering the Azov, the sea has become more saline and therefore less hospitable for the fish that would previously have migrated here to breed. Rising salinity has also meant the arrival of invasive species like moon and barrel jellyfish, the washed-up bodies of which sometimes cover the beach, making it look like another planet.[24] These new arrivals have brought new problems. The now common warty comb jellyfish can eat ten times its body weight every day, hoovering the sea of the zooplankton that others need to survive. These combined factors have transformed this once thriving sea into what some environmentalists are now calling 'a zone of ecological poverty'.[25]

There's another problem for the Azov Sea. On the far side of the bay, in the cordoned-off area controlled by Metinvest, a mountainous land formation dips down into the water. This is the *shlakova hora*, the slag mountain produced by the steelmaking industry that is now one of the city's most iconic landmarks. Sashko tells me that the mountain is such a resonant symbol here that his filmmaking collective sometimes refers to it, tongue-in-cheek, as Mount Fuji, the Japanese volcano, sacred and revered in the Buddhist faith, which was repeatedly reproduced in paint and woodblock by the artist Katsushika Hokusai, among others. Looking across the sea to the man-made mountain today, as the waves crash rhythmically and the white foam dances across the water, I can see what Sashko means.

Slag heaps are special places. Growing up, I would see them from the window of our car as we travelled around the South

Wales Valleys where my mum worked. The coal heaps in South Wales, toxic when they were first created, had neutralised over time and regreened – money from the European Union after industry ended had helped with that process. Later, when I moved to Scotland, I got interested in the 'bings' of West Lothian, the bright orange oil-shale heaps that you can see from the aeroplane window when you're landing at Edinburgh airport. The process that extracts the oil chemically neutralises the shale, making the bings resemble the ecosystems of deserts. Opium poppies of the sort normally found in Afghanistan, whose seeds have been disseminated by migrating birds, grow on them today.

Mariupol's slag mountain has a similar dark romance. The toxic legacy of extractive colonialism and, after independence, community-impoverishing capitalism, it is also part of the urban infrastructural grammar, part of what it means to be from and to belong to this place. Stable in size today, this slag heap wasn't always this static. Before the outbreak of war, subsidiary slag-processing businesses existed at the edges of the metallurgy industry, turning the slag into cinder blocks and construction materials, and using the grit and gravel for roads.[26] Like the bings of West Lothian that were quarried for their useful 'blaes', the red stone flakes used in construction, Mariupol's slag heaps started to shrink. When the market for construction materials crashed and transportation became more difficult after parts of the Donbas region were occupied in 2014, the mountain started to grow again.

Steel slag, a molten complex of silicates and oxides that solidifies on cooling, is produced all over the industrialised world. Where and how it gets dumped, buried or reused, however, is determined by the political system in which it's produced. Recycling of industrial waste is easier in politically stable economies with legal systems that can enforce environmental policies and are not undermined by corruption. In Germany, where industrial lobbies are strong, for example, construction companies are required to use 50 per cent of non-natural raw materials produced by industry, conveniently resolving the problem of waste. In Ukraine, similar laws exist but are not enforced.[27] The requirement that 10 per cent of materials for road construction should come from metallurgy companies is regularly ignored. Construction companies, seeing little incentive to follow these rules, and little consequence in flouting them, prefer to buy gravel cheaper from quarries closer to their construction sites.[28]

On days like today, when the wind whips the beach reeds dramatically first in one direction then the next, it also picks up fine slag particles and scatters them over the sea. This dust combines with the other waste that industry has dumped in the water: petroleum products, coal, brick dust, iron ore and shards of glass. The result is that the Azov Sea is becoming murkier, more granular, more opaque. Today it is a brownish grey, forming a near-monochrome composition with the slag mountain behind and the uniform, heavy greyness of the sky above. But the darkening of the sea is more than just an aesthetic problem. It means that light does not reach plant organisms that oxygenate the water, creating conditions for other life forms to survive. These changing conditions have been linked to the increase in fish kills (localised reductions in fish populations) in the Azov's waters. While fish kills used to be an irregular phenomenon, since the 1960s they've started to happen every year.[29]

Despite the challenges of living both with hyper-polluting industry and in such close proximity to a simmering war, a sense of
radical hope pervaded Mariupol when I visited in 2021. Many
young Ukrainians that I met elsewhere wanted to move there.
It was one of the most exciting cultural spaces in the region,
they told me, with one of the most dynamic activist communities, where people were really making a difference. This local
scene was in part a result of cultural activists moving to the city
from Donetsk and Luhansk after 2014, and it certainly benefited
from international grants that flowed into the city to support
civil-society building initiatives. But it also had its roots in the
post-Chornobyl environmental activist movement, which was
the first to question the social contract between Soviet industry
and the communities who lived with its toxic consequences.
Far from a foreign import, then, resistance to political and
social inequalities was baked into public consciousness.

In 2022, Russia deindustrialised Mariupol in the most violent way imaginable. During a three-month siege that killed tens of thousands of people, it systematically razed the city, destroying 90 per cent of its residential architecture, and obliterating the two giant metallurgy works that had dominated the skyline for over a hundred years. Azovstal was subjected to the worst of the damage. Russia furiously bombed the factory, where civilians were also sheltering, for weeks on end as it attempted to root out fighters from the Azov Battalion and other Ukrainian forces from its bunkers. By the time the city was occupied, Ilych was irrecoverably damaged and Azovstal was in ruins. At the time of writing, an operation to clear the debris is still ongoing at an estimated cost of $8 billion.[30] While Russian politicians periodically declare their intention to restore and reopen the factories, it's widely understood that the damage is irreversible. Large-scale industry in Mariupol is over for good.

As soon as Mariupol was occupied, the Russian propaganda machine began churning out the most sickening kinds of spin about Russia's love and care for the city. Mariupol was twinned with St Petersburg in a perverse act of cultural diplomacy, and a buzz began to circulate around plans to rebuild and revive the city. In early 2023, I saw a piece in the news about a Russian project to adapt the ruins of Azovstal' into a 'leisure zone' that could function as an industrial park or a recreation space. Visitors would be able to wander through the evocative ruins of the site, it explained, to ponder works of contemporary sculptural art and relax in hipster cafés housed in the factory's former warehouses. What's more, thanks to Russia's destruction of the city's metallurgy industries, there was talk of turning the city into a seaside resort. Some estate agents even talked about Mariupol being 'the next Crimea' and encouraged savvy investors to purchase property there before prices went up.[31]

The idea of turning Mariupol into a tourist attraction was not only ghoulishly bad taste but was also delusional, given the disastrous ecological impacts of the war. Ukrainian forces had mined the Azov Sea after 2014 to defend the city from Russian advances, but the three-month Russian siege in 2022 tipped this situation over into environmental catastrophe. A report produced by the Mariupol NGO Razom in 2023 noted that the Azov Sea contained hundreds of unexploded shells and mines, which were gradually corroding and contaminating the water with their heavy metals. A second, even more disturbing source of pollution was the soil that flowed into the water through storm drains, containing bacteria produced by the mass burial sites and chaotic landfills improvised during the siege.[32] While the destruction of the city's steel mills had lessened air pollution, it had created other unanticipated kinds of waste. Without the pumps to regulate its levels, the fluorescent sump water that surrounded Azovstal like a moat had begun seeping into the sea. Combined, these conditions had produced an ecological disaster zone of the most tragic proportions.

When I next saw Sashko, it was at a workshop in Lviv in 2023, and he was no longer comparing his city to Gary, Indiana. 'Now, when we think about our city-twins, we think less about places characterised by heavy industry, like Pittsburgh or Sheffield,' he explained, 'and more about the ones that have experienced urbicide, like Sarajevo or Aleppo.' When a colleague asked him about the post-industrial future of Mariupol, and if there was any hope to be found in its horrific experience, he was silent for a moment in thought. 'We all wanted to live in a de-industrialised Mariupol,' he said, 'but not like this, not with such terrible costs.' His feelings were shared by many others who'd lived with the pollution generated by heavy industry in the east, who'd petitioned politicians to regulate oligarchic owners and coordinated spectacular protest actions that had gone viral on social media. All had wanted, demanded, and willed change to come. But not like this, not with such terrible costs.

SIX

Cultural Front

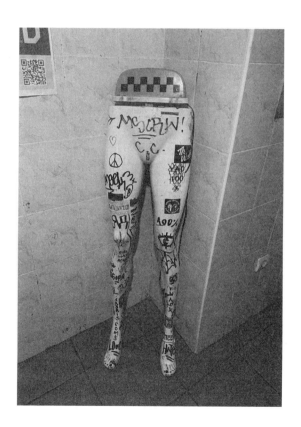

Pokrovsk Local History Museum houses many objects that were discovered on this territory, from the era of the pits and the catacombs to the Scythian-Samarian cultures and Cossack times. Standing next to these exhibits, you feel a deep connection with past generations of people who inhabited these lands – this is surely one of the reasons why it's so important to visit local history museums, to experience that connection.

But our museum is also a resource for building society. After all, the future has to be built on firm historical and cultural foundations. Unfortunately, our museum space is currently closed to visitors and most of our exhibits have been evacuated to safer places, separated from the country whose history and culture they commemorate.

Since the full-scale Russian invasion began on 24 February 2022, my life, like the lives of hundreds of thousands of other people, has been divided into 'before' and 'after'. Uncertainty, fear for our children, displacement, explosions – my fellow Ukrainians have had to learn to live with all of these things. And that's without even getting into how a person should feel who has defended their country from Russian aggression with a weapon in their hands? Or who has lost a loved one in the war? Or has been left with a disability . . .?

Today we are all traumatised by the war, especially those who've seen it up close. War is surely the most terrible thing humanity ever invented, and yet diplomacy and civilisation (and these are relative concepts for me now) have not yet found a way to stop it.

I dream about people returning, buildings being rebuilt, culture being restored, along with education, transport, factories, and steppe ecosystems. I dream about my native land

triumphing over its external aggressors and its internal prob-
lems. And I hope that this evil will not go unpunished, and that
Ukrainians will once more know what it means to be happy.

Anhelina Rozhkova
Pokrovsk, Donetsk region

IN MANY of the eastern Ukrainian towns and villages I visited, there were exhibitions dedicated to the events of 2014. While some of these displays, like the billboard-sized portrait photos of Ukrainian military in Mariupol's City Park, were well funded and state produced, others had been curated spontaneously by local communities. Encountering these memorials was always poignant. They signalled how close the war was in time and space, and how alive it was in people's memories. One exhibition that stayed with me was the work of Andrii Taraman, an activist from the village of Oleksandro-Kalynove in the northern Donetsk region. When Misha and I turned up spontaneously on his doorstep in July 2021, Andrii, who was in the middle of dinner, downed knife and fork to give us a tour, then and there, around the museum that he had almost single-handedly set up and curated.

The exhibition Andrii showed us told the story of Ukrainian village life across the Soviet twentieth century, through independence in 1991, and up to the present day. It opened in a thick-walled, whitewashed hut, decked out in traditional 'peasant' style, immersing its visitor in an idealised world of Ukrainian folk life before transporting them into the politically conflicted twenty-first century. The museum's main exhibition space was in what would once have been the village's House of Culture. On one side of this building's main hall, painted with fluorescent-green Soviet-era paint, Andrii had installed a composition of communist propaganda art salvaged from local decommunisation purges. Here an oil-on-canvas portrait of a ponderous Lenin hung above a silver bust of the same Bolshevik leader, bordered by other grand paintings in socialist-realist style. On the other side of the room, in dialogue with this arrangement, was an installation of objects Andrii had collected in 2014 when the Kramatorsk region had been briefly occupied by Russian forces, before being recaptured by Ukrainian troops in July the same year. Andrii explained that he had fought with the Ukrainian army to push the invaders back during that summer. On his military excursions, he'd collected souvenirs that he thought might be important after the war.

As we wandered around, Andrii directed our attention to one of the objects on display: a road sign pocked with bullet holes that showed the placenames 'Donetsk' and 'Kostiantynivka' next to an arrow pointing backwards on itself. He explained that he had found the road sign while defending his native region and been impressed by its symbolic power: Donetsk had ended up being occupied by Russian military and Russian-backed separatists and cut off from the rest of the country after 2014, while Kostiantynivka had come back under control of the Ukrainian army. Andrii had transported the huge sign with difficulty back to his village. He had installed it there under a large hand-woven camouflage net emblazoned with the Ukrainian trident that he and fellow soldiers had paraded through the streets of Kostiantynivka after its liberation. Speaking about these objects and remembering these events, his voice quavered with emotion. 'One day soon we'll travel back along that road from Kostiantynivka to Donetsk,' he said. Standing in this room full of powerfully resonant objects, I too hoped with all my heart that he was right.

❖

Between 2014 and 2022, the war in Donbas had catastrophic humanitarian consequences. In addition to causing tens of thousands of deaths and casualties, the war displaced more than 1.5 million people, scattering them across Ukraine. Government-controlled Donbas was undoubtedly the region most impacted by the conflict. While some fleeing the occupied territories decided to relocate to major cities like Lviv or Kyiv, many preferred to stay closer to home and settle in industrial centres like Sievierodonetsk, Kramatorsk, and Bakhmut. These newcomers put pressure on underfunded public services, but also brought with them energy and fresh ideas. Among the displaced were many cultural activists, who'd until then worked in Donetsk and Luhansk and were now based in smaller towns, diversifying and enlivening local cultural life. If in the past few Ukrainians had bothered to visit the east, dismissing it as a depressing industrial region with little to offer in terms of attractions, after 2014 it became known as one of the most dynamic and culturally vibrant regions of the country.[1]

This burgeoning activist culture was supported by foreign grants and loans. Travelling around the Donetsk and Luhansk regions, you couldn't miss the red-and-blue USAID plaques and EU signs that hung outside the entrances of restored historical buildings and in the halls of newly established community centres. This money came with conditions, of course. By the time I visited Donbas in 2019, some local organisations and NGOs had become experts in producing the discourse around 'civic society', 'democracy-building' and 'knowledge exchange' that was required to qualify for this funding. But while western capital did support many cultural projects in the east, there was also a healthy degree of cynicism towards the foreign aid landscape and the patronising assumptions that underpinned it. Artists sometimes expressed this cynicism in humorous and subversive ways. I heard about several projects that built faux-humble acknowledgements into their work of the authors' status as 'grateful subjects' in an 'economically underdeveloped' and 'culturally deprived' 'war-torn' region.[2]

When Russia began its full-scale invasion of Ukraine in 2022, one of the twisted justifications for its actions was that western capital and influence had infiltrated the country, turning Ukrainian people against their 'brotherly' eastern neighbour and rupturing historic cultural ties. I even heard some of my own students echo this argument back to me. Could Russia really be blamed for challenging the expansion of NATO to its borders? Wasn't it true that the war in Ukraine was really a 'proxy war' between the US and Russia, and that both sides were using all the military and cultural weapons in their arsenals to win? What these arguments missed, and still miss, however, is the agency and independence of the Ukrainian people. What they assumed was that Ukrainians were empty-headed pawns without political will or vision of their own.[3] Meeting activists from the east, who adeptly navigated political and funding landscapes to realise the projects and goals that they wanted to achieve, revealed a very different picture. Far from remotely manipulated puppets, these were communities with a defined sense of their own identity and a clear vision for their region's future.

◈

In the summer of 2021, I helped coordinate another summer school for artists and researchers in Pokrovsk, formerly Krasnoarmeisk, a mining town around sixty kilometres from occupied Donetsk and an hour's drive from the military border. I travelled to Pokrovsk by car with a friend from Kyiv, and as we approached the eastern city, the roads suddenly turned bad. We slowed to a crawl as we attempted to swerve the massive potholes made by the tanks and other military vehicles that had pummelled the asphalt during the intense fighting in 2014. Slowing down let me study more closely the landscape passing by my window. The thick green of the steppe was regularly interrupted by derelict factory buildings with systematically smashed windows, rows of blast furnaces, and chimney stacks. Coal slag heaps, the region's ubiquitous symbols, looked like geometric pyramids on the otherwise flat steppe horizon.

Arriving in Pokrovsk, we were greeted by Anhelina Rozhkova, the director of the Pokrovsk Local History Museum, the organisation that would be hosting our summer school. Anhelina's team was delivering a press conference about our project to a group gathered outside the brightly painted museum, which since 2014 had become a centre of cultural activism in the front-line city. As we watched Anhelina speak enthusiastically about our work together, my colleague from Lviv told me that she had been appointed to this job from the private sector, where she'd worked for several years in public relations for the mining industry. This professional experience, combined with a passion for local historical knowledge, had provided Anhelina with a nuanced understanding of the industrial history of the Donetsk region. A pride in that history animated her words and lit up her face as she spoke.

After the press conference, Anhelina took us inside the museum to tell us about the history of her home city, Pokrovsk. Like many places in the Donbas region, it had had different names throughout its history due to being colonised multiple times.[4] Before it was Krasnoarmiisk, a Russian placename that referenced the Red Army (*Krasnaia armiia*) in the Soviet period, it had been a railway settlement called Hryshyne. Over the course of the 1880s, Hryshyne had emerged as one of the most important railway-repair centres in the region, attracting labour migrants from across the empire. Yet as geological knowledge of the region's industrial potential grew, and with it, foreign capital investment, the railway industry had gradually been supplemented by coal mining. By the end of the Civil War, when Hryshyne was briefly renamed Postyshevo before its Russian namesake, Pavel Postyshev, was repressed in the

Stalinist purges, industrialists had sunk six mines the area that would become the city. Around this time, a firebrick factory called Dinas had also been also founded.[5] To illustrate this development, Anhelina holds up a hefty terracotta slab, now a museum exhibit, manufactured in the 1930s.

I ask Anhelina about the factory's name, as it's a word that's familiar to me from back home in Wales. Anhelina isn't aware of any link between the two regions, so, suspecting that there might be some connection forged by transnational capital, I decide to do some research of my own. After a bit of googling in my hotel room that night, I discover that Dinas derives from the Welsh, Craig y Ddinas, meaning 'Fortress Rock', a high promontory of carboniferous limestone and silica rock located in Bannau Brycheiniog or the Brecon Beacons in Wales. Dinas silica became the general name for the heat-resistant brick used in industrial furnaces across the world, including in the Soviet Union, and its name was taken for other industrial places, such as the Dinas micro-region in Pervouralsk in Russia's central Sverdlovsk oblast. When I relay my findings to her the next day, Anhelina is delighted. She declares that we must take a trip to the Dinas factory district – a 'lively, more working-class part of town', she explains – as part of our workshop programme later in the week.

Anhelina's enthusiasm for local history and heritage is infectious. It's easy to imagine how she has led so many successful projects in recent years, building around her a community of cultural enthusiasts with an interest in their region and its industrial past. In 2019 she collaborated on a project with the NGO The Museum is Open for Repairs, an initiative run by cultural activists from Lviv with expertise in heritage management that aimed to support museums in the east to rethink their often unreconstructed Soviet-style exhibitions.[6] The project recovered the history of the Ukrainian composer Mykola Leontovych, who taught music and singing for four years at Pokrovsk's School of Railway Workers and came to be best known for writing the ethereal New Year's song 'Shedrik' adapted by the American composer Peter J. Wilhousky into the famous Christmas song 'Carol of the Bells'. Together, Anhelina and the NGO team transformed the museum's main exhibition room into a multimedia exploration of Leontovych's life and times. The project wrote Pokrovsk's industrial history, until then a story with narrow local relevance, into a more expansive narrative of Ukrainian cultural life and its reach around the globe.

In recent years, Anhelina's been working, together with my university, St Andrews, and the Center for Urban History

in Lviv, on a project to digitise Soviet-era industrial photography collections located in museum archives across the east.[7] The museum team in Pokrovsk has uncovered a body of little-known work by Mykola Bilokon and Marko Zalizniak, two photographers who documented industrial life in Soviet Pokrovsk.[8] These photos, which are hung in frames around the museum today, are truly remarkable. While some are typical Soviet-style shots of Stakhanovites clutching the tools of their trade, others capture more intimate unexpected moments: children playing charades with their parents; teenage girls beaming as they dance the flamenco. These are far from the hyper-bleak visions of post-industrial decrepitude and military violence that normally circulate in news about the eastern region. They rather affirm the life, love, and joy that formed part of this city's history, something that is often lost in accounts of repressions, hunger, and violence. Anhelina knows that it is important for people to have heritage that they want to identify with and that inspires them. It is this that forms and sustains community in a region facing such a difficult present.

At our summer school, Anhelina is supporting young artists as they work with the museum's Soviet-era photo collections, adapting and reinterpreting these for new audiences. One filmmaker, Elias Parvulesco, is retracing Bilokon's photographic route around Pokrovsk, filming in the places where his photographs were taken and integrating recorded interviews with the photographer into his visual narrative.[9] In contemporary Ukraine, where Soviet heritage risks being discarded as 'historical trash', this nuanced work with the cultural legacies of the past is important for building bridges between communities. This is part of what Anhelina wants to do through her work at the museum. To create dialogue across generations, classes, and professions in an increasingly fractured political landscape.

Later in the week we go on the promised excursion around the historic Dinas district. Crossing the intersecting railway tracks that are at the centre of the city's origin story, we enter a neighbourhood of folksy wooden houses whose gardens over-flow with fruit bushes and trees. Several of us stop here to fill our mouths and pockets with apricots, raspberries, and juicy fat blackberries that turn our greedy fingers purple-black. But we quickly move on. Anhelina wants us to see a historic water tower that she hopes will be restored as part of plans to raise the visibility of the city's industrial heritage. The tower, a hand-some red-brick building, hoves into view as we walk through thickets so dense that you almost forget you're in a city. On one

of its bricked-out shelves, as if curated, we find a sculptural Dinas firebrick. In the glow of the evening light, it appears almost otherworldly, resonating with some half-forgotten cultural meaning that seems to stretch across space and time.

When Russia invaded in February 2022, Pokrovsk narrowly escaped occupation. It instead remained on the front line of the fighting, constantly under shelling, in a state of permanent emergency. Anhelina decided not to leave her city. As she explained when we next saw each other, she felt that she needed to stay in the community she'd worked so hard to build, whose cultural heritage she'd done so much to preserve. Anhelina and her colleagues packed and evacuated much of their museum collection, including the originals of the photographs by Bilokon and Zalizniak. They even buried objects referencing Ukrainian national themes in undisclosed locations around the city, knowing that these would be particularly vulnerable to attack if Russian soldiers reached the town. In August 2022, missiles fell in Anhelina's neighbourhood, injuring her husband and damaging her block of flats. Later, bombs hit her museum, blowing out its windows and doors. Anhelina stays because, as she explains, some people have to stay. She stays because, in her words, 'Donetsk region is Ukraine and always will be because each of us here believes it to be so.'

❖

Internal displacement is a violence that takes many different forms. It is the forced rupture with the environments, people, and practices that shape one's identity. It is the exhausting task of building one's life over again in a different context, restoring community, friendships, and interests. Even when some kind of stability is restored, its violences can be re-experienced unexpectedly at any moment and with renewed force. My friend, Dima, told me a story that darkly illustrates this precarious state. Displaced from Luhansk in 2014, Dima used to dream of his abandoned family home, of his books and possessions still in his teenage bedroom, of his basketball hoop in the garden that must, by then, have become wildly overgrown. After the full-scale invasion in 2022, this dream became a nightmare. With changes to legislation that allowed for the confiscation of property of displaced residents, his house was seized by Russian soldiers. Chillingly, he was able to observe the soldiers via a CCTV camera that still functioned on the outside wall of the house. He sent me clips of them drinking beer, laughing as they dumped his childhood things on the lawn.

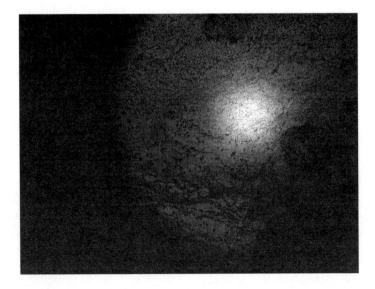

Many of the cultural activists whom I met in the Ukrainian east were displaced people. Among them was Misha Kulishov, whose flight from Horlivka in 2014 was to be the start of a new chapter in his life. Misha had always been interested in the region's industrial heritage, but his experience of the Russian-manufactured insurgency had strengthened his commitment to preserving these vulnerable legacies. Knowing how Russian propaganda could expand to occupy every inch of cultural life had spurred him to support activist projects that countered the toxic myth of the 'Russian World'. While culture in occupied Donbas narrowed after 2014 to a cult of militarism, Soviet nostalgia, and hysterical, media-invented fear of Ukrainian 'fascism', in the government-controlled east it blossomed and diversified.[10] If Putin and his cronies would argue that this was down to the sly creep of Western influence and money into these 'traditionally pro-Russian' lands, displaced activists like Misha would disagree. By waging war in Donbas, displacing its most energetic and innovative residents to non-occupied parts of the region, Russia created its own staunchest political opponents.

One of the fiercest of these was Masha Pronina, an artist, activist, and educator originally from Donetsk. In November 2021, during my stay in Mariupol, I visit Masha at Platforma TU, an arts collective and community space in the city established by her friend, the artist Diana Berg, also displaced from Donetsk in 2014.[11] Joining Diana at TU, Masha had thrown herself into coordinating art clusters for marginalised young people who felt they didn't fit in in their patriarchal local community. When they first started the project, which had a particular focus on LGBTQ+ teens, no one had believed that they would make it work: 'Everyone said that no one would turn up, that there were no young people like that in Mariupol,' she tells me, handing me a black Nescafé in a paper cup. 'But they did turn up. And they were the most incredible, impressive, cool, brave kids you can imagine.' At TU, Masha mentored teenagers in the creative arts, taught them how to make things, install and promote their own artistic work. She also showed them how to write petitions to local politicians, design posters that would go viral on social media, and express their demands in assertive and articulate ways that would make local politicians sit up and listen.

TU is housed in a knocked-through nineteenth-century town house, which Masha explains used to be used as a synagogue, gym, warehouse, workshop, and even, at one time, as an Orthodox church. In one interview, Diana has joked that TU retains something of the building's former sacred status. And, indeed, it's easy to imagine how queer teens who felt alienated by Mariupol's heteronormative, traditional working-class culture could experience something like a spiritual awakening here. Masha tells me about her own art practice. A collage artist who often works with print media, she likes to explore communist legacies, ecological questions, and feminist themes. At TU, one of her collages is on display: a divided cellophane curtain hangs from the ceiling, onto which she's glued fragments of images of communist leaders and their writings taken from canonical Soviet-era texts. The work suggests the unwanted intimacy of the communist past. The cut-out fragments of Lenin's and Stalin's faces leer from the strips of plastic, which resemble a shower curtain. When you pass beneath them, they touch your body lightly, leaving their invisible trace.

TU is one of a number of community art spaces that emerged in the east following the outbreak of war in 2014, propelled by the creative energy of cultural activists displaced from the occupied territories.[12] These hubs of community activism, run by dedicated and talented artists and curators, invigorated cultural life in the region, encouraging young people to think beyond belittling stereotypes that had bracketed them as 'Russian-speaking' (and, by implication, not Ukrainian enough), incurably Sovietised, and culturally underdeveloped, and to imagine instead alternative identities and futures for the region. The social impact these organisations had is hard to understate. The belief that they conveyed in the possibility of political and cultural change was transformative and was rightly feared by Putin and his cronies. As Feemnia, a teenager who took enthusiastic part in the activities at TU, put it in an essay published in 2022: '[TU] was the sort of space that enabled self-expression, a space where you could do anything and everything. Literally EVERYTHING, that is within the bounds of the law . . . You want to learn how to make collages? Sure, go ahead! You want to play the guitar? The speakers are next to the stage. Want to organise a witches' coven? Let's have a think about how we can make that happen.'[13]

Back in Mariupol, Masha is giving me a tour of TU's exhibition space, located on a first-floor mezzanine looking down over the open workroom below. On the walls are works produced by the collective's young artists on the themes of 'Loneliness' and 'Life Beyond the Factory'. Many of the artworks are powerful portraits of the interior lives of the young people, others are reflections on the outside world and its various challenges. A work by sixteen-year-old Anastasia

Timchenko includes a drawing of a disproportionately large girl, crouching and withdrawn on the steps of a busy cultural centre in Mariupol. Next to the image a note reads 'this work shows the state when you are physically present in society, but emotionally absent'. A more Mariupol-specific video work by seventeen-year-old Denys Barabash plays at the edges of black comedy, depicting the teenage artist as a factory labourer gradually drinking away his work-related depression. Masha is filled with pride and respect for this new generation of Mariupol artists. 'We have a really cool team,' she says, 'people from Donetsk, people from Mariupol, it's all one big family, we're all friends and we all support one another, and, as I always say, working at Platforma TU is my dream job.'

When Russia started bombing Mariupol in February 2022, Masha and friends from TU made the difficult decision to relocate to western Lviv, where displaced children were pouring into the city. I talked to her a few weeks after the move. Speaking in a voice that was cracked with tiredness and emotion, she explained her decision: 'We didn't want to leave Mari. We didn't want to leave our families. It was incredibly difficult for us,' she explained. 'But we thought we had to go somewhere where our skills could be of use, where we could do art therapy with children and be part of a team that could carry out this important work.'

Many of the teenagers who formed the TU community remained behind in occupied Mariupol, lacking the means or the agency to relocate elsewhere. Masha describes their acts of bravery with angry pride: one left his shelter during a missile strike wearing the rainbow flag and sang the national anthem, she tells me, another started filming the shelling, making posts

about how people in the city survived during the siege. She hopes that some of the skills that TU has taught them will help them navigate the experience of Russian occupation: 'These amazing queer – and not only queer – kids, these new kids, this new generation, new Ukrainians, we're so proud of them,' she says. 'We would always say that this generation will change our country, that the fact that we have kids like this now . . . well, that they were going to make our country so strong . . . And then the Russians came and attacked us, attacked our kids . . . and I can tell you this, one of our kids, one of our Ukrainian teenagers, is worth ten thousand of those orcs, so Putin can go fuck himself.'

The outbreak of war in 2014 didn't only displace individuals. Entire cultural institutions, universities, museums, and art galleries were also forced to relocate. Displacement did not mean an end to their existence, however. Universities in exile from the occupied territories re-established themselves in new locations, delivering lectures online for students who were now scattered across Ukraine. Galleries and museums had to search for new premises from where they could continue their curatorial activities. Those with the best contacts landed in relatively comfortable new conditions and were able to secure grants and collaborations to support their work. Others experienced more difficulties and had to settle for empty units in shopping centres. Many struggled to navigate the new landscape of domestic and international funding that was supposed to support their cultural adjustment.

During our summer school in Pokrovsk, I talked to Dmytro Bilko and Kateryna Filonova, researchers at the Donetsk Museum of Local History, which had been displaced to Kramatorsk in 2014. The museum had lost almost all its collections when Donetsk was occupied by Russian military and fighting groups, and the pair had made use of innovative crowdsourcing methods to repopulate its archives. Integrating digitised materials from museums and archives with connected histories, including the Glamorgan Archives in Cardiff, which held materials relating to the nineteenth-century Welsh labour migration to the city, the museum had gradually regained its status as a regional hub of historical knowledge and expertise. In 2022, however, when Russia began bombing Kramatorsk, the museum was forced to evacuate again. This time, Dmytro decided that the only real way to defend his country's cultural heritage was to join the Ukrainian territorial defence.

Another Donbas organisation displaced in 2014 was IZOLYATSIA: Platform for Cultural Initiatives, a contemporary arts and community centre formerly located in Donetsk.[14]

IZOLYATSIA took its name from the insulation factory that had housed it. This had been the property of its director Lyubov Mikhailovna's industrialist father, one of the last Soviet-era 'red directors', who had made his fortune in the early years of capitalism. Mikhailovna was a mythological figure at IZOLYATSIA. Her money and connections allowed things to happen there that could not have happened anywhere else. I once experienced this power when I helped organise a workshop with the Platform in 2019. When the delay with the transfer of funds from the UK meant that we were too late to purchase train tickets to Donbas, Mikhailovna made some calls. As we panicked that our workshop would be a disaster, cogs were already in motion behind the scenes. The next thing we heard, an extra carriage had been added to a train, allowing our group to travel comfortably to the east.

IZOLYATSIA was a major player in the cultural life of government-controlled Donbas.[15] Its projects were smartly conceived by a collective made up mostly of displaced curators and practitioners who understood the power dynamics of delivering cultural programmes in the war-impacted region. I ended up being friends with some of the people who worked at the organisation. Dima Chepurnyi, displaced from Luhansk in 2014, was a Kyiv-based programme curator at IZOLYATSIA who led the coordination of our summer school in Sievierodonetsk in 2019. Working with Dima, I was struck by his collaborative approach, how he made sure to partner with local community groups in the region rather than parachute ideas in from the better-resourced capital city. While tensions could still emerge between activists who lived and worked in the region, closer to the front line, and the displaced curators and managers now working out of Kyiv, this practice of continuous dialogue and interaction was surely what made IZOLYATSIA's work so successful.

Misha Kulishov was also affiliated with IZOLYATSIA. Learning about his extensive knowledge of industrial history and heritage, curators at the Platform invited him to become an on-the-ground facilitator for their 'Grounding' (*Zazemlennia*) project in 2020. 'Grounding' was a radical new departure for the Platform. It involved the partial relocation of the centre's cultural activities back to Donbas, and specifically back to the salt-mining city of Soledar. When I visited Soledar with Misha in August 2021, the project was just beginning to take shape. Several artist's residencies had already taken place in the city and a small new premises painted in IZOLYATSIA's signature grey-and-orange colours had opened in the centre. Inviting me inside, Misha showed me a small exhibition of work by the Donetsk artists Andrii Dostliev and Lia Dostlieva, who had licked a salt lamp in the shape of a tank to a nub, one lick every day, a comment on the embodied experience of military violence.[16] In another corner was a small library of books about art and IZOLYATSIA's past projects. Beanbags were stacked up against a wall, ready to be deployed around the room for events.

Misha explained that the Soledar artist-residents had come from different regions of Ukraine and that some had been nervous about exoticising the already heavily exoticised region in their work. Some had asked to be introduced to local groups and practitioners with the aim of working with them to create artwork that could be meaningful in a local context. Misha showed me the result of one of these residencies. Roksolana Dudka, a mural artist from the Poltava region whose work made use of folkloric ornaments and motifs, had designed two beautiful decorative boards that covered the windows of Soledar's then-derelict House of Culture.[17] The brightly coloured murals, featuring exotic, blooming plants and hovering insects, popped cheerfully from the grey walls of the abandoned Soviet-era building. Misha told me that Roksolana wanted to make artwork through the residency that would bring joy to local people by brightening up the urban environment. Looking at the simple and heartfelt project, it was hard to imagine that it failed to achieve this goal.

While travelling in Ukraine, I had the chance to talk to other artists who had made work as part of IZOLYATSIA's Soledar residency. Tetiana Pavliuk and Irena Tischenko were relative newcomers to the Ukrainian art scene and so had been surprised when they'd been selected for the prestigious scheme. With an interest in themes of environmental and ecological damage, the pair had made work that responded to Soledar's history of salt mining. When I met them in Pokrovsk, they explained how Misha had helped them find places near Soledar that were visibly marked by the industry, where they'd made video installations featuring a billowing strip of scarlet cloth. Tetiana told me that confronting Soledar's current difficulties, the contracting salt industry and destabilising impact of the war, had made the artists think differently about their work and adopt a more collaborative approach. The final stage of their project had involved working with local school-children, who'd helped them fill fish bowls full of salt, artificial blood and sand; a creative reflection on the ways that humans had impacted on local ecosystems.[18]

Back in Soledar, Misha wants to show me another local initiative located in a different part of the city. Cutting through

the Park of Recreation, filled with Soviet-vintage fading graphic art and crumbling ornaments, we arrive at a newly mown football pitch. I realise that it's been a while since I've seen another living soul and ask Misha why the city is so deserted. 'It's hot,' he answers laconically. Not everything has political significance, it seems. Misha gestures to a brick building on the edge of the pitch, the outside wall of which is painted with the face of a Rasta DJ in headphones next to the words 'NOT EVERYTHING IS SO SIMPLE'. This is the headquarters of the creative studio 'Radio Dja', he tells me, a community music group run by young people from Soledar. Misha knocks and a man in his early twenties lets us in, clearly delighted that Misha's dropped by. As our host rushes to find clean cups to fix us some tea, I take a look round this hub of local community activism.

The building's entranceway is decorated with hundreds of 1990s cassette tapes that have been stuck to the walls like tessellating tiles. Another wall is painted with guitars, drums, video cameras, and games consoles and the words 'Radio Dja' in rainbow paint. Entering the main practice space, the first thing I notice are the overlapping knotted-pile rugs that cover the concrete floor. Given the heavy-metal music that the group in the room is currently practising, these rugs give the space a slightly incongruous feel, as if we've wandered into some metal-head grandma's front parlour. It soon becomes clear, however, that this is a place where these young people spend a lot of their time. It makes sense, then, that they've decorated it like a home from home. After passing me my tea, one of the group's founders tells me about Radio Dja's activities. With support of some small grants, they've created a space where teenagers can learn to play instruments and any local band can record their tracks for free. In recent months they've even set up a small amateur film studio where those who are interested can make their own documentary and feature works about the city.

Radio Dja is a genuinely grassroots initiative. Driven by local activists who want to change the cultural profile of their front-line city, it is an example of the political agency of the Ukrainian people that's so often ignored in media discussions about the 'proxy war' in Ukraine. Groups such as this might have received support from foreign funders, but this did not make them mindless puppets of US ideologues bent on turning the region against Russia, as Putin would have it. Young people in Soledar didn't need USAID to tell them that Russia's influence on their lives was toxic, or that the Russia-instigated war, which has drained their region's resources and made it vulnerable to military aggression, had also stolen their opportunities for the future. As I leave Radio Dja, I spot a whiteboard on the wall on which some community members have brainstormed

ideas for what they do and don't want for the future of their city. In the 'want' column are some achievable goals: more tourism, more green space, more culture. In the 'don't want' column there is just one entry: fighting.

In January 2023, Russia devastated Soledar with missiles and artillery as it attempted to encircle Bakhmut to the south. President of Ukraine Volodymyr Zelenskyy, in one of his TV addresses, solemnly commented on conditions in the city, saying 'the situation there is very difficult – there is almost no wall left standing'. In drone footage that I watched on YouTube, the city resembled Dresden after the Allies' bombing of 1945. Soledar's salt mines were being used as hideouts for Wagner mercenaries, wave upon wave of whom had been released against the city. Watching the unfolding horror, it seemed that Russia's disproportionate use of force was almost vindictive. It seemed that Putin was punishing this peaceful industrial town for aspiring to be something other than a war-compromised, economically deprived periphery, a place where markets for salt had dried up and future prospects were bleak. Soledar is, at the time of writing, still under Russian occupation, its buildings devastated and its population mostly displaced. If and when Ukraine gains back control of this city, it will need a fleet of artists painting brightly coloured boards to cover its smashed windows, and an army of heavy-metal-loving activists to return music, song, and dance to the local community.

I remember talking to a friend from Belarus about activist life in Ukraine. It was after the 2021 mass protests that had attempted to oust Aleksandr Lukashenko, and my friend's mood was low. 'If only we had the tenacity of the Ukrainians, we could force a revolution too,' he'd complained. 'But people back home don't have the same radical hope that something can change, that a different future is possible.' While I disagreed with my friend, who seemed to underplay the bravery of his compatriots, it appeared true that Ukraine, with its multiple revolutions and uprisings, was an outlier among other former Soviet states that had often struggled to free themselves from the shackles of Russia's postcolonial influence. In recent years, Ukrainian friends had even begun to mythologise this revolutionary mentality, linking it to the nation's ethnic ties to the Free Cossacks and their stubborn refusal to be ruled by outsiders. But while easy to romanticise, the strength of Ukraine's civil society could also be explained more prosaically, as a result of neoliberalism and state withdrawal. When funding for public services had been slashed after 1991, many government responsibilities had been offloaded onto volunteer organisations and NGOs.[19] In the absence of strong public institutions, Ukrainians had had no choice but to take matters of politics into their own hands. The Orange Revolution and Maidan had been expressions of that desperation.

There was a phrase for this in the Ukrainian east: *delat' nechego*, or *robyty nichoho* in Ukrainian, which translates roughly as 'there's nothing else for it'.[20] *Delat' nechego* was what happened when unregulated capitalism resulted in mass unemployment and a crisis in public services, and when Russia brought war to your doorstep. It was a strategy of resistance, of taking matters into one's own hands, and a means of controlling one's own fate. This sentiment was what drove the activist organisers in Pokrovsk, Mariupol, and Soledar to harness the resources at their disposal to make a difference to their local communities. It was also what explained the huge wave of self-organisation in Ukraine that followed Russia's full-scale invasion in February 2022. When Russia escalated the war, museum directors knew not to wait around for the state to issue official instructions about their evacuation, and volunteers knew not to look to the authorities to organise convoys of cars to transport people from the occupied territories or get humanitarian aid, food, and medicine to those who couldn't leave. The rapid mobilisation of the Ukrainian people, which took the world so by surprise following the invasion, was the result of a hard-learned lesson taught by years of living with wartime precarity and state weakness. And after 2022, activists in Donbas were some of the best placed to deliver these lessons to those living in parts of the country less used to war.

SEVEN

Big War

There's a little town in the Luhansk region called Almazna. Or perhaps it would be more accurate to say that it's a workers' settlement. Almazna is a suburb of Kadiivka and it's where the railway station Stakhanov is located. I often visited Almazna as a kid to see my grandparents. On the train there you'd see those typical Donbas landscapes from the window: fields, steppe that had been transformed into clusters of industrial towns and villages, slag heaps, and little forests scattered through the ravines.

When you travel by train to Almazna, you pass by the soda factory in Lysychansk. At the end of the journey, you see the huge burning torch of the iron-alloy plant on the horizon – that's how you know that you've arrived. I often went cycling with my grandad and cousin along the Almazna ravine. There's a forest there. It's an incredibly beautiful place where you can see hundreds of old oak trees. A stream flows through the entire ravine. It used to be a river, but no one can remember its name. And somewhere in the depths of the forest there's an old stone bridge that crosses the stream. It was built more than a hundred years ago.

It sometimes seemed like time had stopped there, it was so quiet. Even the echo of the trains arriving at the station couldn't disturb the sense of peace. The noise dissolved into the ravines and the hills of Old Donbas, the only reminders of which were the ancient stone buildings and the slag that was scattered along the roads. For me, Donbas is these very landscapes, where instead of the hum of industry, you can hear the steppe winds and the murmur of water in wells, where you can shelter in the forest from the 40°C summer heat and listen to the crackle of the coals that your grandfather's burning in the stove in winter.

These native lands of mine have been occupied by the Russian Federation since 2014. I've visited my grandparents several times *since then, making a huge detour to cross the checkpoint at Stanytsa-Luhansk before driving halfway across the region to arrive finally at their house sixteen hours later (the railway line that Stakhanov was on was discontinued in 2014 and the station abandoned. Before, it only used to take two hours). But each time I visited, I never went far into the forest. Local people said that Russians had set up a training camp there and that it was dangerous. Sometimes, when I went walking along the ravine, I could hear bursts of machine-gun fire. I consider this forest a place of power, and after the occupation, I felt as though something had been stolen from me. Now with the occupation of the whole Luhansk region, this feeling has only grown stronger.*

Oleksandr Kuchynskyi

Sievierodonetsk (occupied since 2022)

IN AUGUST 2023, eighteen months after the start of the full-scale Russian invasion, I crossed the Polish border by bus into Ukraine. I was travelling to attend a workshop on public history that I had helped to organise in western Lviv, and was excited to be seeing friends from the east again, many of whom were now displaced across the country. Since my last visit to Ukraine in November 2021, so much had changed. While, as frustrated Ukrainian colleagues pointed out, February 2022 was not 'the beginning' of the war but the escalation of an eight-year-long Russian invasion, no one doubted that this was something serious and new. Responding to my frantic texts in April 2022, Misha, my cave-exploring friend, had described his experience of being displaced a second time in just ten years: 'You know, it's easier the second time than the first, but this war is different,' he'd written. 'This is big, the biggest war that Ukraine has ever experienced. Nothing will ever be the same again.'

'Big war' (*velyka viina*), 'the full-scaler' (*povnomashtabka*) – many new terms had emerged to describe what Ukrainians were living through after February 2022. In the first disorientating months of the invasion, Russia had advanced simultaneously on multiple fronts. From Belarus in the north, troops had forced their way as far as the Kyiv region, occupying the surrounding towns and villages, terrorising local populations. When the Ukrainian army had driven the invaders back from the capital, Russia had concentrated its military operations in the south and the east. The world had watched with horror the devastating siege of Mariupol in spring 2022, Russia's bombing of the drama theatre where children were sheltering, and its merciless shelling of the 'green corridors' meant to allow civilians to evacuate the city. If Mariupol had lodged itself in the world's imagination as a site of appalling atrocities, many more brutal acts of urbicide had followed: Bakhmut, Sievierodonetsk, Marynka, Rubizhne, Volnovakha, Lyman, Izium. Russia had razed them all.

By the time I crossed the Polish border in the summer of 2023, Ukraine was experiencing the fastest growing displacement crisis since World War II. By the end of 2022, nearly one in three Ukrainians had been forced to leave their homes. An estimated 5.9 million people had been internally displaced, while over 5.7 million refugees had crossed the border to Central and Western Europe.[1] Under the weight of this human traffic, border crossings had become notorious sites of communal suffering. On the cloudless August day that we crossed, we waited ten hours on the Polish highway in the pounding

33°C heat, with no shade aside from that cast by our stationary FlixBus on the baking tarmac. I watched as Ukrainian tweens whiled away the hours weaving flowered headdresses from dandelions and recording synchronised TikTok dances next to the central reservation. In the background of their videos, rows of lorries transporting camouflaged tanks could be seen, waiting their turn to enter the country.

Arriving in Lviv much later that day, I'd been excited to reacquaint myself with the city. Making the most of the hour that remained before the midnight curfew – in place since February 2022 as part of martial law imposed across the country – I'd ventured from my hotel to the old centre. As I walked, I took in the boarded-up monuments, whose signs, installed by the local authorities that had evacuated them, read 'the originals of these artworks will be returned after our victory!' and the churches, whose windows were stacked with sandbags. Despite the late hour, Lviv seemed busy, frantic even. People were gathered in small groups around benches, chatting and shouting, and couples promenaded through the warmly lit streets holding hands. As I wandered back to my hotel, a group of giggling young women overtook me. Above them, attached to the wrist of the group's bride-to-be leader, a helium-filled, smiling condom-balloon bobbed gently in the sky.

Since the beginning of this war, journalists and commentators have eulogised the 'resilience' of the Ukrainian people. From orchestral performances during blackouts to art exhibitions in bomb shelters, Ukrainians have been praised for their superhuman abilities to preserve their cultural identity in the face of Russia's brutal attacks. But the language of resilience can itself be a violence, which as Palestinian scholar Malaka Shwaikh notes, imposes 'supernatural coping mechanisms onto communities struggling with adversities, romanticising them as exemplary in enduring injustices, [and] obscuring their humanities'.[2] Encountering Ukraine again after eighteen months of war, seeing how people continued their lives in spite of the violence, I too felt an instinct to project heroism onto these everyday realities. Meeting again with colleagues from the east whose efforts had helped preserve aspects of cultural life from the region, I had to try not to romanticise, and rather see this work as necessary acts of resistance to Russia's ruthless war of cultural erasure.

❖

'It's difficult to understand the war from Lviv,' a friend from Kharkiv is telling me over Zoom some days before I leave. 'It's become more like a party town since the start of the full-scale invasion. The city's full of visitors seeking a bit of respite from the war.' And it's true that Lviv, a historic Galician city bursting with impressive old architecture and picturesque squares, does feel oddly touristic. The city's terraces are packed with lively groups snacking on pizza and sipping iced coffees. Market stalls heave with soap from the Carpathian Mountains, pyramids of honey jars, and paper bags full of Lviv's signature aromatic black coffee. I hear foreign-accented English everywhere in the city centre, usually in dialogue with English-speaking Ukrainian guides, explaining some aspect of local culture. Street vendors line the central Market Square, offering services and requesting money from passers-by. One vendor approaches me and offers to take my photograph with a vintage-looking folding camera. She explains to me that she'll print the image on a page of sepia newspaper featuring other random items of 'olde worlde' Lviv news.

But to my eye, so unaccustomed to this war, the conflict is also everywhere I look. Standing at a pedestrian crossing, I watch a rotating billboard scroll through its adverts: between face creams and dairy products, a poster for a film about Oleksa Dovbush, a Robin Hood-like folk hero from the days of the Polish-Lithuanian Commonwealth, flicks up, with the tagline 'Live here freely, on your own land!' It's followed by a pencil drawing of a screaming female face beneath the words 'Don't be silent' and a QR code linking to psychological support services for women impacted by the war. On the second day of my trip, as I'm wandering through Lviv's less touristy industrial district in search of a new art gallery that turns out to be closed, I enter a children's spiritual centre to ask for directions. In the centre's cool and shady assembly hall, two women weaving camouflage nets on a large loom look round at me in surprise. I wonder how many other people across the city are right now involved in similar everyday tasks to support the war effort.

Lviv, which felt so far from the war in Donbas before 2022, now reminds me of eastern Bakhmut or Kramatorsk, which I visited in 2021. There is a precariousness to the easy-going atmosphere here, which can easily be shattered by the howl of the air-raid siren, even if most Ukrainians ignore them by this point. While Lviv remains a fiercely proud, Ukrainian-speaking city, the arrival of thousands of displaced people to the region since the start of the invasion has altered the cultural landscape. If it is still rare to hear Russian spoken in the city – rarer than ever now the language has become toxified by the war – I overhear some snippets of conversations that suggest the tensions that the displacement crisis has caused. A woman on the street speaking strongly accented Russian to a man explains that he has to wash his own dishes while he is a guest in her home. The war has broken many homes apart and forced new, not always harmonious ones, to form.

The day before our workshop I take a walk to the memorial for the Heavenly Hundred, a reference to the civilian participants killed during the 2014 EuroMaidan protests, which is located on a hill overlooking the city's rooftops. The memorial has been constructed in the form of a monumental barricade and uses steel produced by Mariupol's Azovstal works before it was annihilated by Russian bombs in 2022. A separate section of the memorial honours those who died in the occupied territories after 2014. Fruit trees have been planted and tags tied around their trunks marked with personal details of the war

heroes. I walk out onto one of the elevated platforms that looks out over the city and notice that someone has sellotaped a flyer to the glass balustrade. The flyer has a number to call for those who have lost their homes, have no means to support themselves, who are alcohol or drug dependent. 'It is always possible to start again,' it reminds its potentially desperate reader.

On the evening of the second day of my trip, I realise that I have not yet heard the wail of the air-raid sirens that Ukrainian friends say now haunts their dreams. I've been studying the Lviv Air Raid Alert app that I was told to download before coming to the city, and I know that they happen on average once or twice a day, so it seems strange that I've gone this long already without hearing one. With a sense of slight foreboding, I fold some presentable clothes that I could wear in the hotel shelter, if necessary, before going to bed that night. I already feel slightly self-conscious of my foreigner jumpiness:

Ukrainian friends have explained that Lviv is too far from the 'hot war' for anything dramatic and unexpected to happen. Even if missiles were fired in the city's direction, they tell me, people would have at least an hour to get prepared.

At 4 a.m. I'm woken by the siren's undulating howl. I put on my clothes and descend the stairs to the hotel's shelter, a basement floor with narrow changing-room benches, which is accessed through the breakfast room. The only other person in the shelter is a Czech hotel guest I've briefly met in the lift. He is clearly embarrassed by his own jumpiness and declares performatively in Russian, 'There's no need for this!' before heading back upstairs. I wait on my own for an hour, wondering why the 'all clear' siren, which normally sounds after thirty-five minutes, has not yet happened, before sleepy Ukrainian families begin to file into the brightly lit basement. I hear a couple saying that they heard an explosion from the hotel window. Another is tracking the hits across the city: four, five, six. I feel the hair on my arms standing on end. Lviv has only experienced one relatively minor strike since the beginning of the invasion: the situation seems unreal. Despite the terror, my Ukrainian neighbours are calm – chatty, even. Is this the resilience journalists have been writing about? Lying sleepless in my hotel room after we've been allowed back upstairs hours later, it feels to me more like the awful normalisation of something that should never have to be normalised.

There are no more missile strikes on Lviv, but I spend a lot of time in shelters along with other nervy foreigners. During one air alarm, I chat to a Nepalese woman working for an international NGO providing emergency medical aid. She tells me that in eastern Dnipro the alarms would sometimes

sound after the first missiles had hit. Her Ukrainian colleagues got used to going to shelters only after they heard the first explosion. With a dozen or so alarms each day, it would be impractical to go each time one sounded: no one would ever get any work done. She tells me that she stayed in her room during the strike the previous day, balled up in a corner of the bathroom with pillows all around her. From the sixth floor she had felt the hotel shake with the explosions. She said that it had felt like a major earthquake in Nepal.

When Russia first started bombing Ukraine back in February 2022, everyone had been this nervy. With bombs raining down on all the major cities, and air defences not yet in place, people had been prisoners in their basements, metro stations, and cellars. Sasha Kuchynskyi, my artist friend from

Sievierodonetsk, had written to me from the city to say that the situation there was tense. Russia was firing its notoriously imprecise Soviet-era Grad missiles at the city, and the Ukrainian army was fighting back with their artillery. Before the internet went down in Mariupol, friends had sent texts and pictures from their shelters, describing the constant explosions across the city, the lack of food and water, the pervading sense of dread. In Melitopol, colleagues had spent days in cellars and basements before fleeing the city by car, driving through bombing in a convoy of vehicles with dipped headlights, the night sky lit up behind with toxic oranges and reds. The hair-raising fear that I felt for just one moment in my hotel shelter had been a mass condition for Ukrainians for many months, years even. The cost of all of this 'resilience'? Chronic fatigue, high blood pressure, stress, anxiety, trauma, and many other long-term health problems that were only now beginning to make themselves known to medical professionals across the country.

Yevheniia (Zhenia) Kalugina, director of the Sloviansk Local History Museum in the Donetsk region, is telling me about her experience evacuating her museum collections as we sit, eating cheesecake, in one of Lviv's central cafés. Sloviansk, where she has remained throughout the invasion, has been battered by shelling as Russia has fought frenziedly to gain control of the whole of the Donetsk region. Gesturing at the hipster décor of the café in which we sit, Zhenia drops her voice and tells me that Ukraine is now two countries: the one where war is happening, and the one where it isn't. Grabbing her phone, she begins showing me photographs of a dead toddler pulled from the rubble of a house in Sloviansk some weeks earlier, the distraught father desperately pressing his ear to the child's chest. I find it excruciating to look at the image, particularly here, in this cheerful setting. This is another kind of 'resilience' that Ukrainians have been forced to develop – the practice of consuming ubiquitous images of death.[3]

Zhenia suggests that we visit her friend, Olha Honchar, another museum director, originally from Brovary in the Kyiv region, who has now been appointed head of the widely acclaimed Territory of Terror Museum in Lviv. I know from watching presentations online that Olha has also been a key figure in the evacuation of museum collections from the east, many of which were looted or destroyed by Russian forces, and I am keen to meet her in person. We arrive by taxi at the museum, an impressive complex of buildings located on the territory of a former Jewish ghetto and transit prison located in the decidedly untouristy north of the city. Olha greets us warmly at the entrance and apologises that she only has time for a quick guided tour before she jumps on a train to Poland in a quest to obtain her US visa. In her capacity as museum spokesperson and lobbyist for cultural heritage, she is off to New York in search of funding to realise the institution's future ambitious plans.

The museum is a collection of intersecting national traumas: the Famine, known in Ukraine as the Holodomor (1932–3); the Stalinist Terror (1937–8); Ukrainian occupation and collaboration in the Holocaust; and now Russia's full-scale invasion. We walk through rooms of carefully curated exhibits: a wagon standing on rails outside the main museum building holds a wall of suitcases, some open and spilling out personal

belongings, and a card index with details of the Jewish individuals and families deported from this prison. Inside, the
rooms are divided by walls constructed from archival boxes.
The suggestion is that the past is tidied away in museums and
archives such as this and that it is the responsibility of the
engaged citizen, of us museum visitors, to drag it into the light
and scrutinise it, to question its underpinning assumptions.
We end our tour at a table piled with photographs from different periods and places in the Soviet past. Pictures of groups
on skiing holidays in the Caucasus in the 1970s lie on top of
school photos of kids in 1980s Lviv with comically large white
school-uniform pompoms in their hair. 'Which of the individuals in these images are perpetrators and which are victims?'
Olha asks, provocatively. This question is more controversial
than ever now, as opinions in the country polarise, often along
generational and class lines, about Ukraine's entanglements
with Soviet power.

In a separate museum building – a long wooden barracks
that would once have held Jewish prisoners – the question of
who the perpetrators are is unambiguous. Here a less curated,
less polished display of objects collected from the recently
de-occupied territories explores Russia's manipulation of
the truth about the war. One table is covered with propaganda posters, flyers, and newspapers that were distributed
throughout occupied towns and villages around Kyiv. A leaflet
featuring a Russian soldier in army fatigues, fighter jets in the
background, declares: 'Our Actions Are Just. Victory Will
Be Ours!' A Russian newspaper distributed around occupied
Kherson offers advice about how to return to Kherson 'from
Ukraine', where to study, and how to receive your pension.

On the opposite wall is a display of uniforms belonging to dead Russian soldiers. Next to each uniform is a letter from a Russian schoolchild, copied neatly onto graph paper, that was found among the soldier's belongings. The letters earnestly thank the soldiers: 'Without your bravery and valour we would not be able to live,' one reads. 'We all believe in you, love, and admire you.'

Zhenia and Olha discuss the complicated politics of museum funding in Ukraine and their efforts to preserve and promote the collections of the more precarious museums in the east of the country. When Russia redoubled its assault on the Donetsk and Luhansk regions in 2022, both women risked their lives packing and transporting Scythian coins, stone babas (anthropomorphic statues found in the steppe belt of Europe), and other unique items of cultural heritage from the regions, saving a historical record of life in the east from pillaging Russian troops. The already chronically underfunded museum sector received little support or guidance from the Ukrainian state concerning emergency measures to be taken to evacuate their collections.[4] Even though Sloviansk, like other towns in the east, had been besieged and briefly occupied by Russian-backed fighting groups in 2014, no policies had been put in place for this eventuality. Clearheaded professionals, like Zhenia and Olha, had been left to make the call on whether or not to evacuate their collections by themselves.

We exit the barracks and wander into the back garden of the museum complex, where a curious scene confronts us. Along the garden's left-hand wall, partially obscured by a living carpet of sprawling grapevines, is a row of Soviet monumental frieze sculptures. The sculptures' heads, where these are still attached, are buried in the verdant wall of vines, their torsos and feet sticking out at an angle, as if they are sunbathing. Together with both an enormous Red Army Soldier and a Motherland sculpture – now prone on their backs – that we passed on our way in, these sunbathers once formed part of the sculptural composition the 'Monument of Military Glory of the Soviet Armed Forces' (1970) by Lviv sculptors Emmanuil Mysko, Dmytro Krvavych, and Yaroslav Motyka, dismantled in 2021. Another corner of the garden is occupied by an eclectic collection of dismantled Soviet World War Two monuments, including a mother and soldier monument in the biblical pietà style. Olha explains that these have all been removed from their pedestals in Lviv in recent months, following the intensification of decommunisation processes across the country.

A former transit prison seems a symbolically fitting place for these disgraced monuments, the cultural worth of which is now being hotly debated by heritage professionals in Ukraine. Olha believes that Soviet heritage such as this should not just be erased from view but should become a reference point for public conversations about Ukraine's colonial entanglements with Russian and Soviet cultural legacies. Having these conversations now is difficult: Russia's violent assaults against Ukraine have intensified feelings of alienation from Soviet culture and Russian language, with many Ukrainian native-Russian speakers choosing to switch to Ukrainian as a political act, and having little tolerance for the idea of any kind of a shared history and heritage. If these monuments are in transit, then, it is not yet certain in which direction they are travelling. Perhaps, as part of the reviled legacy of Soviet rule, they are destined to disappear completely into the vines,

to vanish from view and from future public debate; the next generations may never even know they were there.

I am sitting with Sashko Protyah, my filmmaker friend from Mariupol, Sasha Kuchynskyi, and my American friend, the artist Clemens Poole in a cult Lviv bar called Traven, listening to them debate which city in the east the owner of the bar comes from. Sashko thinks that Traven was founded by a guy displaced from Luhansk. The cool DIY aesthetic – furniture upcycled from flea markets (Sasha tells us that his parents had the exact same sofa with the exact same upholstery in the flat he grew up in), retro Soviet crockery, and colourful Post-it notes advertising vegan snacks and beers – speaks distinctly of the region. The name Traven, meaning May, references the owner's revolutionary politics, Sashko tells me, directing my attention to the handwritten posters for music events planned for 1 May. With Labour Day, like other national holidays, cancelled following the introduction of martial law in 2022, it's now up to bars like this one to observe the structure of the festive calendar.

Sasha, who looks much leaner and stronger since the last time I saw him, tells us that he is thinking of joining the army. With the war entering its nineteenth month, and Russia conscripting from a population three times larger than Ukraine's, he is part of a growing number of young people who feel they need to do more to help their country. Clemens also knows friends from Kyiv who've signed up, one of whom, a fellow artist, is now recovering in hospital from a spinal injury that has caused his legs to atrophy. Sasha hopes that the visual and digital skills he's developed through his artistic practice will make him a good fit for air reconnaissance or drone flying. This is far from an easy option. Drone flyers spend long hours sitting in laybys near to the front line, using 3D headsets that give them aerial views from the drones they're flying, and often suffer with motion sickness and chronic fatigue. Drone operators, some of the deadliest fighters in the war, are also key targets in Russian attacks. Their presence in any area they're working in must be carefully concealed.

Sashko advises Sasha to download a course from Prometheus, an online Ukrainian-language platform that provides free skills training in areas from IT to business management. Since the beginning of the full-scale invasion, the platform has been offering courses tailored to the needs of a society at war: among the most popular right now are basic first aid, stress management, and proficiency in business English. The course Sashko recommends deals with the basics of modern military training. In ten parts, it takes students through topics including communication in the battlefield, tactical medicine, and the handling of explosives. Sashko tells us that he's been following the course, even if he finds the language of mechanical engineering alienating as someone more used to working in the arts and filmmaking. Listening to this conversation, I find myself thinking again about the resilience people talk about in connection with Ukraine. Is resilience taking online courses that teach you how to tourniquet a leg torn apart by an exploding mine? It seems like the wrong word.

Sashko tells us about the filmmaking and volunteering work that he's been involved in since he was displaced from Mariupol in 2022. We've just attended a screening of one of his newest films, *My Favourite Job* (2022), which documents the work of volunteer drivers shuttling between the occupied territories and government-controlled Ukraine, evacuating people trapped in the east.[5] In one of the film's most memorable scenes, volunteers sit around a table in the half dark, talking and smoking. Yura, one of the film's driver-protagonists, recounts with manic laughter the violence he's experienced at the hands of Russian border guards and the horrific scenes he's witnessed, including a pitch-black story about a family who buried their dead grandfather with the keys of the car they wanted to evacuate in still in his pocket. The scene is an honest portrayal of the ways in which trauma is processed, how it's experienced as a complex of competing and sometimes contradictory emotions, from black humour to raw, desperate sadness. As I tell Sashko this, the siren starts to wail again outside the window. No one around the table seems to register the sound.

As we leave Traven, with me itching to get back to my hotel shelter and everyone else dawdling in the balmy warmth of the summer evening, Sashko tells me that he's got to go to

the outskirts of the city to help unload a *busik*, an affectionate term his volunteer community use to refer to the Transit vans that arrive from Europe carrying boxes of donated goods and equipment for displaced people. With winter already in their sights, members of his volunteer group are once more think- ing of the basic necessities people will need to keep warm and fed, particularly given Russia's terroristic targeting of energy infrastructures, resulting in blackouts and energy outages. Not for the first time, I wonder what Ukraine would do without the remarkable volunteer networks that supplant the state in so many areas of social and cultural life. The citizen-as-volunteer model, which crystallised in Ukraine following independence, remains fundamental today. Museum workers like Zhenia, activists like Sashko, and drivers like Yura all form part of this continually unfurling societal legacy: people doing it for themselves in the absence of any other viable alternative.

The workshop is intense in a way academic events normally are not. Scholars who work on European cultural memory – the politics of commemorating and memorialising difficult history and heritage – are more used to discussing these things from a safe distance, not from the midst of ongoing violence and trauma. While the social and cultural impact of the Holocaust and Holodomor continues to resonate across generations, carried in the bodies of those descended from the murdered, its genocidal violence is not ongoing at this moment in time, or at least not in the same way. The discussion that I'm observing in Lviv is different. The person on stage is talking about the politics of memorialising the Russian massacre of civilians in Bucha, a small city forty-five minutes' drive from Kyiv, which was liberated in April 2022. The speaker describes the unexpected challenges the local council has been experiencing as the city has turned into a dark tourism attraction. Busloads of Ukrainian visitors, driven by morbid curiosity or a more abstract need to experience first-hand the worst of Russia's violence, turn up each week to this previously relatively little-known town.

The presentation is even more affecting since I have just come from coffee with Oksana Semenik, who was herself trapped in Bucha, where she lived with her partner, while these atrocities were taking place. In the plant-filled café where we meet, we do not discuss her traumatic experiences, but earlier that morning, I read an article that she's written describing the fifteen days she spent in a shelter before deciding to walk twenty-two kilometres past Russian checkpoints to safety.[6] Oksana is an art historian who has become famous on Twitter for her threads decolonising 'Russian' art history, that is, pointing out that many artists who were previously assumed to be Russian were in fact Ukrainian or other nationalities.[7] Speaking to her, I learn about her current project, a book about Ukrainian art produced in response to the Soviet-engineered Chornobyl nuclear disaster. Our conversation helps me understand how the lived experience of war informs Ukrainian scholarship. In Oksana's case, it has strengthened her resolve to promote Ukrainian art and cultural heritage, things that are now threatened in the realest sense by Russian bombs and missiles.

As the workshop's seminars end for the day, I suggest to Misha Kulishov, who has joined us in Lviv from Kyiv, where he now lives with his family following their displacement from Bakhmut, that we get a drink somewhere in the old centre. While I've been in touch with Misha regularly since the invasion began, we've not seen each other since our excursions around the salt mines and gypsum quarries of the Donetsk region two years before, in the summer of 2021. As I introduce Misha to a colleague over a glass of wine and try to explain the impact that his work in the Donbas region has had on my own research, I find myself becoming choked. Misha, for whom these places mean so much more than they do for me, whose professional life and passions were all interwoven with this region, now half destroyed and toxified by Russia's horrific war, takes up the conversational slack: 'All the places that we saw are gone now,' he explains. 'Victoria had an exclusive tour.'

Misha and I leave the beautiful art-deco building where our workshop is taking place and wander through the city's busy streets. I sense that he is mildly irritated by Lviv's touristic buzz as we pass by one packed-out terrace after another in search of somewhere to sit. We end up at Lviv's historic Arsenalna Square: a lively courtyard where Staroevreiska (Old Jewish) Street meets the city walls. Today the square is dominated by a sprawling, fairy-light-spangled terrace belonging to the Trout, Bread and Wine restaurant, owned by a trumpeter, a watchmaker, and a clock mender. But before World War II it was the heart of the city's Jewish community, who made up around 32 per cent of the population. Back then it was overlooked by the Golden Rose Synagogue, a sixteenth-century building combining Gothic and Renaissance styles, built for private use and, later, the main house of worship for Lviv's Jewish community. The synagogue was desecrated and destroyed, along with more than forty others in the city, by Nazi occupiers and Ukrainian paramilitary groups and collaborators during World War II. Until 2016, all that was left of it was unkempt ruins.

My first visit to Lviv, in the summer of 2016, had taken place during the opening of the Space of Synagogues, a new memorial complex on the site of the destroyed temple. The memorial had at that time prompted some controversy. Far-right elements had objected to the implication that Ukrainians had collaborated in the genocide, citing the ulterior motives of foreign (German) sponsors of the project and their desire to shift blame for the mass murder onto Ukraine. Prominent members of the local Jewish community had also, somewhat surprisingly, opposed the project. Arguing that the memorial turned the site into a graveyard, some had even launched legal proceedings to have the project stopped, advocating instead for the full reconstruction of the Golden Rose.[8] In the end, the memorial, which included the preserved synagogue ruins and an installation of thirty-nine dark grey tablets inscribed with writings by Jewish residents and images of pre-war Jewish life, was opened to the public. Taking part in the heated conference discussions that had accompanied the memorial's opening, I remember thinking how alive twentieth-century history was in this part of Europe.

At that time, I could not have guessed that Ukrainians themselves would become the victims of cultural genocide. While by 2016 the war in the east had been simmering away for two years, it was impossible back then to imagine the urbicide and cultural destruction that would follow the full-scale invasion in 2022. As we walk through the historic square, past teenagers perched on the grey stone tablets drinking lemonade, still unable to find seats of our own, Misha tells me about the articles he's been publishing about the historic buildings in Bakhmut that have been razed by Russian missiles.[9] One of the articles is dedicated to Bakhmut's Palace of Culture, a grandiose,

Stalin-era project that was intended to demonstrate the superiority of Soviet architecture over that of Russian tsars.[10] I remember visiting the Palace with Misha and his friend Natalia and her little girl on a sticky summer's night back in 2021. The security guard had let us inside so that I could take a peek at the grand interior. Natalia's daughter had been fascinated by the slowly melting salt sculptures that were on display in the high-ceilinged entrance hall. In September 2022 it had burnt completely to the ground following a Russian missile strike.

Forced to move far away from the mines and factories around which he's built his life and career, Misha is now spending time developing online tours of these out-of-reach places, giving people a chance to see, if now only virtually, the region's awe-inspiring industrial landscapes and infrastructure. One project that he's been working on since the war escalated is a 3D tour of the salt mine in Soledar that we visited together in the summer of 2021. Misha's extensive photography of the mine had allowed him to create a virtual reconstruction of the site even before the invasion.[11] Using the arrow buttons on a computer you can now navigate your way along the salt mine's sparkling corridors, stopping to take in the salt carving of the mine's folkloric spirit Shubin, the salt chapel, and its sanatorium. This suspended reality of the mine's past co-exists with the awful current reality of the mine's occupation by the Russian military. The industrial labyrinths I wandered around, enchanted, with Misha, are now inhabited by mercenary groups responsible for some of the worst atrocities and acts of vandalism in this war.

Strolling back across Arsenalna Square, I wonder what will happen to all of these destroyed industrial places if and when Ukraine gains back control of the eastern territories. It seems unlikely that they'll be treated with the same reverence as the Golden Rose, even if they did form defining places of work, and latterly, following the contraction of industry, iconic landmarks for the local community. Who will build back Azovstal when that would mean it would once more pollute the air and the Azov Sea? Who will invest in the reconstruction of Toretsk's coal mines, which were already ailing to the point of being almost unworkable before the war? Who will clear the slag heaps of landmines so that BMX bike riders can once more pull risky stunts on their slopes? What will be next for the gypsum mines-turned-champagne cellars beneath Bakhmut once the mercenary murderers who now occupy them have been expelled? Will the many voices that witnessed the violence, including those who had to stay under occupation, be represented on stone tablets like they are in Lviv? Whose voices will be missing, purposely left behind in the bloodstained past?

◈

I step off the overcrowded and overheated tram in front of the Lychakiv military cemetery. Colleagues at our workshop have told me I should visit Lychakiv to see how communal rituals of patriotic mourning are interweaving here with the raw grief of intimate, familial loss. At first, I am confused by what I'm seeing. The graveyard, a sea of colourful military banners and flags blowing gently in the wind above a patchwork of decorated graves, takes up just a small corner of a large empty field bordering the Soviet-era Field of Mars memorial. Rather than ceremonious and patriotic, it looks small and somewhat lost in this undeveloped stretch of grey, like a memorial on an industrial estate. I quickly realise, however, the gravity of the scene. Urban planners have had to confront, and prepare for, the worst possible eventuality when demarcating land for this new graveyard. Despite the patriotic talk everywhere of imminent victory, room has been accounted here to accommodate up to another ten burial grounds the size of the one that's currently occupying the right-hand side.

It's true that in Lviv the war does feel far away, despite the recent air strike and the ever-present military messaging. But in Lychakiv it could not feel closer. I walk up the path between the graves, reading the names and dates on the memorial plaques hanging from the crosses. Each grave is a lovingly tended garden, bursting forth with flowering plants and decorated with ornamental stones. Many of the graves are surrounded by wrought-iron lamps and religious figurines. Some are strewn with bouquets of fresh flowers. On the low wooden benches next to each grave, couples and individuals sit, heavy with grief. No one here looks economically privileged: military service is most attractive to low-income groups, and hardest to avoid for those without higher education. The intersection of socio-economic and military violence, which makes Ukraine's most vulnerable the most common victims of this war, suddenly overwhelms me with sadness. I haven't cried in Ukraine until now, but now I cry. Thankfully, this is the right place for it and no one gives me a second look.

When I later tell Zhenia about my visit to the graveyard and about my tears, she looks at me askance: 'We have a hundred graveyards like that in Sloviansk,' she says. 'The whole place is a graveyard.' Comments like this, which I've heard many times from friends in the east, divide Ukraine into two countries: one where the war is happening, one where it is not. The hierarchy of suffering in Ukraine will be one of the most difficult hurdles to surmount in the country's future. Convincing residents of Kharkiv or Kherson that citizens of western Ternopil or Lviv also suffered in this conflict will be hard, just as building solidarity and trust between communities who experienced occupation and those who escaped it will be a struggle. Nor will this simply be a question of 'east versus west', as much of Ukraine's history has been simplistically rendered. Right now, the east *is* the west and the west *is* the east. Many intersecting factors – economic privilege, education, mobility, neurodiversity, as well as, more obviously, language and ethnicity – will have determined people's decisions to move, near or far, or to stay. 'Resilience' will have meant many different things to different people, and far from any of it will be heroic or romantic.

◈

When Misha and I eventually found a table to have our drink, we ordered many different glasses celebrating our reunion. I told him how this evening reminded me of the dégustation we had shared in the ArtWinery cellars located in Bakhmut's gypsum caves. Sitting beneath a folksy sculptural composition in white stone of scantily clad antique revellers gorging on wine, we had sampled sparkling Crimean reds, some of the last batches to be bottled after the peninsula was illegally annexed in 2014, sweet, popping pinks, and prestigious bruts. As often happened now, our cheerful nostalgia quickly tinged with sadness and turned to darkness as Misha told me about watching recent videos of members of the mercenary Wagner group in those same Bakhmut caves, boozing and gloating over the Ukrainian wines. Colonial wars like Russia's do not just occupy physical territory – they also occupy the territory of memory, turning reminiscences into ashes, nostalgia into nightmares.

As we get up from our table to leave, a large insect buzzes past our faces. With a familiar gesture, which recalls the deft way that he caught hawkmoths and other insects for me to look at while we were walking on the Donbas steppe, Misha cups his hands around the creature and draws it in. Opening his grip for me to see, he announces that it is a *bohomol*, a praying mantis. The mantis escapes Misha's grasp before circling back and landing on his T-shirt, printed with the words 'I'm Ukrainian'. I've never seen a praying mantis before, and this moment, like so many others I experience in Ukraine, somehow feels laden with symbolic meaning. I later read praying mantises are thought to be oracles that can predict the future, and in some African traditions they are believed to bring good luck to those they land on, or even bring the dead back to life. No insect will bring the dead back to life in Ukraine, and the fate of the occupied, toxified territories of the east remains uncertain. The knowledge that lives in the person, however, that moves his hand to the insect, gently revealing its twitching head, is harder to destroy. This is what lives on in people, resilient.

Afterword

A year has now passed since I raised a glass with Misha and friends in Lviv. Russia continues to assault Ukraine on a daily basis, targeting children's hospitals, residential buildings, and energy infrastructures in a war of terror aimed at breaking Ukrainian morale.

I write this afterword from a café in Uzhhorod in the Ukrainian west, where a routine blackout has just plunged us into darkness. Like the air-raid sirens in Lviv, these daily blackouts are the new normal: my neighbours don't even look up from their iced coffees and computer screens, which up-light their faces like campfire torches. The pop music that's been playing on a loop is abruptly replaced by the mechanical thrum of a generator outside, one of hundreds in the city, which together form an oppressive urban soundscape. Yet despite these mundane indignities, subtly destabilising everyday life, morale here is far from broken. Workarounds are constantly being found to allow life to continue in spite of everything. I am amazed when my taxi driver in this mountainous region turns up driving a fully electric Nissan Leaf, until he tells me that he charges it with domestic solar panels, part of an EU-funded energy resilience campaign. War has also engendered new kinds of eco-patriotism: turning off lights, taking short showers, and even peeing outside has become more than a statement of one's ecological credentials. It is now an act of military resistance.

If Ukrainians refuse to be broken by Russia's terrorism, two-and-a-half years of war have nevertheless taken their toll. Travelling round the Zakarpattia, Ivano-Frankivsk, and Lviv regions in the west, I speak to many train passengers, shopkeepers, and waiting staff, whose chatty small talk suddenly veers, seemingly involuntarily, into accounts of profound and heartbreaking suffering, of sons and daughters fighting on the front line and of relatives hundreds of miles away struggling to make new lives in some cold and wet European country. These encounters leave me speechless and useless to console. I find myself able only to echo back their words: 'strashno' ('awful') and to hold their tearful gaze. Buildings in this area have largely remained intact, as missile strikes here are rarer, but the same cannot be said of bodies. Sitting on a terrace in Uzhhorod, I watch two men in wheelchairs with bandaged legs try to navigate the pavement's uneven asphalt. Later, a group of ex-soldiers in their battalion's military fatigues sits down to dinner; each has a new prosthetic limb.

I ask a Ukrainian friend if people ever talk about the end of the war. It's the wrong question and a long silence follows.

'What end can we talk about?' she answers eventually. 'The collapse of Russia? Putin's death? Anything else would be impossible. This is an existential war.' I try to hold this problem in my mind but it keeps flip-flopping. The war needs to end but the war can't end. It can't end but it needs to end. This immobilising thought contrasts sharply with the 'nothing else for it' mentality of my activist friends in Ukraine tirelessly raising funds, manufacturing drones, coordinating aid deliveries, and helping people to rebuild their homes. Talking to them, I am once again inspired by their strength of resolve and their clarity of purpose. This is the Ukraine that must lead the rebuilding process after the war; the Ukraine that has so much to teach the rest of the world about ethical practice, community collaboration and social care. This is the Ukraine that I love, and that will allow the country to survive this terrible chapter in its history. This is the Ukraine we must support.

There are many wonderful organisations helping communities impacted by Russia's war in Ukraine. Please consider donating to the following:

- Freefilmers: https://help-freefilmers.network/
- KHARPP: https://kharpp.com/
- Livyj Bereh: https://livyj-bereh.org/Donate-index
- Ukrainian Nature Conservation Group: https://uncg .org.ua/en/

Acknowledgements

This book grew like *solonets* or marsh samphire from the rich sedimentary layers of local knowledge that came before it. Like *solonets*, I understand the book as an extension of this knowledge, something that renders it more visible, rather than depleting its resources. I am so very grateful to all of the knowledgeable, inspiring, caring, and generous people who opened for me the rich history and heritage of Donbas, guided me around this region's special places, and shared their stories about what it means to come from this beautiful part of the world.

My first acknowledgement must be to my friend Mykhailo Kulishov, whose encyclopaedic knowledge of the Donbas region's industrial history and heritage is surely unparalleled in Ukraine, and, thus, in the world. I am indebted to Misha for his long-term, dedicated work researching this region's entangled industrial legacies, which has resulted in a huge archive of literature, cartography, and visual media that proved an essential resource for me when writing this book. Misha was my guide during excursions around the northern Donetsk region and introduced me to many of the places and people about which I write in these chapters. I have no doubt that the trust people showed me, the frankness with which they discussed their lives and the challenges they faced, was due to the fact that Misha, for whom they had enormous respect, was by my side during many of these meetings.

I am also grateful to the many museum professionals, historical enthusiasts, community archivists, art activists, factory workers, and taxi drivers, who shared with me their experiences and personal stories. Anhelina Rozhkova and her team from Pokrovsk; Kateryna Siryk and Oleksandr Kuchynskyi from +/- Art Residency in Sievierodonetsk; Artem Bereznev, Andrii Prokopov, Sashko Protyah, and Masha Pronina from Mariupol; Yevheniia Kalugina from Sloviansk; Natalia Zhukova from Bakhmut; Kateryna Filonova from Kramatorsk; Vitaly Matukhno, Mykola Lomako, and Mykola Skuridin from Lysychansk; Dmytro Chepurnyi and Oleksandr Chekhmenev from Luhansk; Viktor 'Corwic' Zasypkin, Kornii Hrytsyuk, and Dmytro Bilko from Donetsk – thank you for demonstrating the critical care with which communities of practitioners can work with the difficult heritage of industry and the potential these legacies hold for sparking new creativity.

For their collaboration and friendship, I am grateful to my colleagues at the Center for Urban History in Lviv: Iryna Sklokina, Sofia Dyak, Anastasia Kholyavka, Oleksandr Makhanets, Natalia Otrishchenko, Viktoria Panas, and others. The Center for Urban History models ethical, community-engaged practice and has been a source of inspiration for me concerning the ways we can do research differently, producing knowledge with and for those to whom it matters most. For his guidance, generosity, and critical engagement with this book I am indebted to Volodymyr Kulikov. Inspiration for this book was also sparked by conversations with many brilliant researchers of Ukraine, including past and present PhD students and postdocs at the University of St Andrews: Darya Tsymbalyuk, Viktoriia Grivina, Diána Vonnák, Taras Fedirko, and Leyla Sayfutdinova. I am also grateful to my brilliant editor, Marigold Atkey, and the team at Daunt Books Publishing, and my wonderful agent Sophie Scard who helped find this work such a welcoming home. Finally, I could not have written this book without the love and support of my dear friends Anna Lordan, Emily Finer, Kate Cowcher, Clemens Poole, and Shura Collinson. David Hill, thank you for the feminist solidarity, for caring for our home and our daughter while I was away. Oona Donovan, you are a source of joy and light in a world that can sometimes feel dark and scary.

The time and resources spent researching and writing this book were supported by many generous funders. I am grateful to the Royal Society of Edinburgh for their Small Research Grant that got the ball rolling on this project; Arts Council Wales, which sponsored my archival explorations into the history of Hughesovka; and the Scottish Funding Council's Global Challenges Research Fund and Ukraine's House of Europe programme, which supported collaborative work with museums in the Ukrainian east and provided funds to organise two summer schools in Sievierodonetsk and Pokrovsk. I am sincerely thankful to the Arts and Humanities Research

Council, whose funding gave me the privilege of time to write this book and the pleasure of working together with two brilliant postdocs in St Andrews.

The arguments and ideas presented in this book were developed in conversation with colleagues all around the world, thanks to many generous invitations to present work at seminars, conferences, and in public lectures. I am grateful to Dace Dzenovska and the Emptiness team in Oxford; Maja and Reuben Fowkes and the SAVA team at UCL; Juliane Fürst and the Perestroika From Below team in Potsdam; and many other colleagues who extended invitations to speak at research and cultural institutions in Austin, Bridgend, Columbus, Edinburgh, Glasgow, Houston, Kyiv, Los Angeles, Lviv, Narva, New Haven, New York, Oberlin, Oxford, Pokrovsk, San Diego, Sievierodonetsk, Stirling, and Washington. I am conscious of the huge privilege I hold to travel widely, speaking about this research, while many of my collaborators in Ukraine are unable to leave the country due to martial law. It is my honour to share their work and creativity with audiences abroad. I know that their stories have moved many people. Thanks to those, especially those from Ukraine, who approached me after talks to share their emotional reactions to these materials and stories of their own.

This book is for my inspiring, generous, knowledgeable, brave and fierce friends from the Ukrainian east. I dearly wish you a speedy return to your de-occupied homelands, to once more feel the feather grass passing through your fingers and the steppe sun upon your backs.

Notes

PREFACE

1 Darya Tsymbalyuk, 'Erasure: Russian Imperialism, My Research on Donbas, and I', *KAJET* (2022), https://kajetjournal.com/2022/06/15/darya-tsymbalyuk-erasure-russian-imperialism-my-research-on-donbas/.

2 Mykhailo Kulishov, 'Materialy kruhloho stola "Staroho rudnyka"', in *Kryvoluts'ki chytannia – 2023: Mynule, vidrodzhene viinoiu. Liudy, ob'ekty, podii.* Zbirnyk istoryko-kraeznavchykh prats' (Kharkiv: Machulin, 2023), pp. 229–30.

3 Olena Stiazhkina, 'Donbas ne povernet'sia v Ukrainu, bo Donbasu ne isnue', *Ukrains'ka Pravda*, 3 November 2014, https://www.pravda.com.ua/columns/2014/11/3/7043067/.

4 Oleksiy Danilov's statement was made at the forum 'Electoral Reform: Estimation through the Values, Political Rights, and Quality of Procedures' on 24 March 2021, in Kyiv. See National Security and Defense Council of Ukraine (2021), 'Oleksiy Danilov: The Functioning of the State in the Territories of Donetsk and Luhansk Regions Controlled by Ukraine is Fully Ensured', 24 March 2021, https://www.rnbo.gov.ua/en/Diialnist/4857.html.

5 Denys Kazanskyi and Maryna Vorotyntseva, *Yak Ukraina vtrachala Donbas* (Kyiv: Chorna hora, 2020), pp. 311–12.

6 *Ibid.*, p. 311.

1. MINERAL WORLDS

1 Darya Tsymbalyuk, 'Pamiat' vuhillia', *Korydor: zhurnal pro suchasnu kul'turu*, 29 February 2020, http://korydor.in.ua/ua/stories/pam-iat-vuhillia.html.

2 The following biographical details are taken from the entry 'Evhraf Petrovich Kovalevskii, *Russkii biograficheskii slovar*': *v 25 tomakh* (St Petersburg-Moscow, 1896–1918), v.9, pp. 22–4.

3 Mykhailo Kulishov, 'Kovalevskii E. P. Petrograficheskaia karta Donetskogo gornogo kriazha, prostiraiushchegosia po Bakhmut-skomu i Slavianoserbskomu uezdam Ekaterinoslavskoi gubernii i po Miusskomu nachal'stvu zemli Voiska Donskogo, sostav-lennaia na osnovanii nabliudenii i otkrytii 1823 i 1827 godov', *Shakhty i rudnyki Donbasa*, https://www.donmining.info/2016/07/kovalevskiy-petrograficheskaya-karta-donetskogo-gornogo-kryazha.html.

4 Evhraf Petrovich Kovalevskii, 'Geognosticheskoe obozrenie Donetskogo gornogo kriazha', *Gornyi zhurnal* (St Petersburg: Tipografiia ekspeditsii zagotovleniia gosudarstvennykh bumag, Knizhka 1, 1829), p. 30.

5 A. Sliusarev, *Priroda Donbassa: Kraevedcheskie ocherki* (Stalino: Stalinskoe oblastnoe izdatel'stvo, 1955), p. 14.

6 *Ibid.*, p. 27.

7 Serhii Lymans'kyi, *Viddilennia Ukrainsk'oho stepovoho pryrodnoho zapovidnika 'Kreidova Flora'* (Ukrainian Nature Conservation Group, 2018).

8 A. Sliusarev, *Priroda Donbassa*, pp. 13–15.

9 Artwinery Museum, Bakhmut, 'Istoriia Artemovskogo zavoda', July 2021.

10 V. D. Simonenko, *Ocherki o prirode Donbassa* (Donetsk: 'Donbas', 1977), pp. 35–6.

11 I. O. Levakovskii, *O slavianskikh soliarnykh ozerakh* (Trudy Obshchestva ispytatelei prirody pri Imperatorskom Khar'kov-skom universitete, 1869, T.1.), p. 1.

12 M. V. Kulishov, O. V. Drogomirets'ka, Ya. V. Sinitsia, *Shliakh, poznachenyi silliu. Solona istoriia Skhodu Ukrainy* (Kramators'k: Drukars'kyi dim, 2022), pp. 8–9.

13 Evhraf Petrovich Kovalevskii, 'Geognosticheskoe obozrenie Donetskogo gornogo kriazha'.

14 Darya Tsymbalyuk, 'Pamiat' vuhillia'.

15 V. V. Riumin, *Chto takoe kamennyi ugol'* (Kharkiv: VSSR, 1921), pp. 1–7.

16 See, for example, V. I. Podov, *Otkrytie Donbassa: Istoricheskii otcherk. Dokumenty* (Luhansk, 1991), pp. 96–9; and, V. I. Podov, *Istoriia Donbassa. Donbass v XVII–XVIII vekakh* (Luhansk: Al'ma-Mater, 2004).

17 The words are reproduced, for example, in Evhraf Petrovich Kovalevskii's nineteenth-century geological treatise, 'Geognosticheskoe obozrenie Donetskogo gornogo kriazha', p. 1.

18 M. M. Lomako and M. V. Kulishov, 'Poshuky vugil'noi balky Skeliuvatoi v okolytsiakh Bakhmuta', *Grani istorii: zb. Nauk prats. Spetsial'nyi vypusk – materialy II Vseukrains'koi naukovo-praktichnoi konferentsii 'Bakhmuts'ka starovyna: kraeznavchi doslidzhennia* (Slovians'k, 2018), Vip. 1(9), pp. 90–92.

19 Asia Bazdyrieva, 'No Milk, No Love', *e-flux*, 127, May 2022, https://www.e-flux.com/journal/127/465214/no-milk-no-love.

2. COLONIAL ENTANGLEMENTS

1 Tetiana Portnova, 'Landshafty Donbasu', in *Pratsia, vysnazhennia ta uspikh: promyslovi monomista Donbasu*, ed. by Iryna Sklokina and Volodymyr Kulikov (Lviv, 2018), pp. 48–9.

2 William Sunderland, *Taming the Wild Field: Colonization and Empire on the Russian Steppe* (Ithaca: Cornell University Press, 2004), p. 62.

3 Hiroaki Kuromiya, *Freedom and Terror in the Donbas: A Ukrainian-Russian Borderland, 1870s–1990s* (Cambridge: Cambridge University Press, 1998), pp. 11–33.

4 V. D. Simonenko, *Ocherki o prirode Donbassa* (Donetsk: 'Donbas', 1977), pp. 91–93.

5 Oliva Irena Durand, '"New Russia" and the Legacies of Settler Colonialism in Southern Ukraine', *Journal of Applied History*, 12 December 2022, pp. 62–3.

6 Sunderland, *Taming the Wild Field*, pp. 4–5.

7 V. I. Podov, *Otkrytie Donbassa: Istoricheskii otcherk. Dokumenty* (Luhansk, 1991), pp. 17–19.

8 *Ibid.*

9 Mykhailo Kulishov, 'Torske ozera. Chertezh gorodam ukrainskim i cherkasskim ot Moskvy do Kryma (okolo 1670 g.)', *Shakhty i rudnyki Donbasa*, https://www.donmining.info/2018/11/1670-torske-ozera-chertezh-cherkasskim-gorodkam.html.

10 Podov, *Istoriia Donbassa*, p. 35.

11 Michael Khodarkovsky, *Russia's Steppe Frontier: The Making of a Colonial Empire, 1500–1800* (Bloomington, Indiana: Indiana University Press, 2004), pp. 221–9.

12 Aileen Friesen, 'State Violence, Mennonite Settlers, and Structures of Power in the North Caucasus', unpublished conference paper presented at 'The Imperial Plow: Settler Colonialism in the Russian Empire and the Soviet Union', Yale University, 1–2 May 2023.

13 Podov, *Istoriia Donbassa*, pp. 44–6.

14 Marlene Laruelle, 'The Three Colors of Novorossiya, or the Russian Nationalist Mythmaking of the Ukrainian Crisis', *Post-Soviet Affairs*, 32, no. 1 (2016), pp. 55–74.

15 Durand, '"New Russia" and the Legacies of Settler Colonialism in Southern Ukraine', p. 67.

16 *Ibid.*

17 Podov, *Istoriia Donbassa*, pp. 101–4.

18 Oleksandr Rybalko, 'Pro nadazovs'kykh grekiv ta ikhni movy', *Mariupol's'kyi park pam'iati*, 2023, https://www.mariupolmemory park.space/library/nadazovski-greky/.

19 Wim Peeters, *Stal' u stepu* (Kyiv, 2010).

20 John P. McKay, *Pioneers for Profit: Foreign Entrepreneurship and Russian Industrialization, 1885–1913* (Chicago & London: University of Chicago Press, 1970); P. V. Ol', *Foreign Capital in Russia* (New York and London: Garland Publishing Inc., 1983); and *Inostrannoe predprinimatel'stvo i zagranichenye investitsii v Rossii. Ocherki*, ed. by I. V. Bovykin (Moscow: Rosspen, 1997).

21 Volodymyr Kulikov, *Pidpryiemstva i suspil'stvo v zavods'kykh i shakhtars'kykh poselenniakh Donbasu ta Pridniprov'ia v 1870–1917 rr.* (Kharkiv: Vid-vo KhHU imeni V.N. Karazina, 2019). On the risks of international investment in the Russian Empire at this time, see J. P. McKay, 'Cockerill in Southern Russia, 1885–1905: A Study of Aggressive Foreign Entrepreneurship', *The Business History Review*, 41:3 (1967).

22 Victoria Donovan, 'Vitannia z Iuzivki! Lystuvannia brytans'kykh migrantiv ta pryv'iazanist' do mistsia v industrial'nomu land-shafti Donbasu v kin. XIX – poch. XX st.', *Histor!ans.ua*, 06 January 2020.

23 Theodore H. Friedgut, *Iuzovka and Revolution: Life and Work in Russia's Donbass, 1869–1924* (Princeton, NJ: Princeton University Press, 2014), pp. 39–71.

24 J. N. Westwood, 'John Hughes and Russian Metallurgy', *Economic History Review*, 17, 3 (1964), pp. 564–9.

25 Theodore H. Friedgut, 'Labour Violence and Regime Brutality in Tsarist Russia: The Iuzovka Cholera Riots of 1892', *Slavic Review*, 46, 2 (1987), p. 246.

26 Friedgut, *Iuzovka and Revolution*, p. 72.

27 Donovan, 'Vitannia z Iuzivki!'

28 McKay, *Pioneers for Profit*, p. 36.

29 Peeters, *Stal' u stepu*, p. 8.

30 Volodymyr Kulikov, 'Industrialization and Transformation of the Landscape in the Donbas Region (Late 19th – Early 20th Century)', in *Migration and Landscape Transformation. Changes in Central and Eastern Europe in the 19th and 20th Century*, edited by Heidi Hein-Kircher and Martin Zuckert (Göttingen: Vandenhoeck & Ruprecht, 2016), pp. 57–81.

31 McKay, *Pioneers for Profit*, p. 42.

32 These ideas were articulated by, among others, the Russian chemist and inventor of the periodic table, Dmitrii Mendeleev. See, for example, D. I. Mendeleev, 'Budushchaia sila, pokoiashchaiasia na beregakh Dontsa. Mirovoe znachenie kamennogo uglia i Donetskogo basseina', *Severnyi Vestnik* (August–December, 1888).

33 D. Grushevskii, *Imeni Il'icha: iz istorii ordena Lenina Zhdanovskogo zavoda imeni Il'icha* (Donetsk: Izd-vo 'Donbass', 1966), p. 4.

34 Iu. Ia. Nekrasovskii, *Ognennoe stoletie, 1897–1997* (Mariupol: PMTs MK 'Azovstal', 2009), pp. 5–7.

35 *Ibid.*, p. 7.

36 Valentyna Lazebnyk, *Stal' u stepu. Pohliad z Ukraini. Istorychni narysy* (Dnipro: 'Art-Svit,' 2017), pp. 108–110.

37 Nekrasovskii, pp. 8–9.

38 L. P. Morozov, *Mariupol' na vidovykh otkrytkakh. Illiustrirovannyi katalog, 1898–1917 g.g.* (Mariupol', 2009).

39 'History of the Company', Azovmash, https://www.azovmash.com/en/history.

40 Mary Louise Pratt, 'Arts of the Contact Zone', *Profession* (1991), p. 34.

41 For more on the history of Stoupky, see *Stoupky: Chetvertoe izmerenie, 1881–2018*, ed. by Svetlana Ovcharenko (Kramatorsk: 'Pechatnyi dom', 2018) and *Stupki i gollandskaia solianaia shakhta 'Petr Velikii'. Stroeniia i te, kto zhil i rabotal tam*, ed. by Hanneke, Hariett, and Olga van den Muyzenberg, trans. by S. Ovcharenko and N. Zhukova (Bakhmut: Stichting Van den Muyzenberg-Kiessler, 2013).

3. CULTS

1 This note was inspired by an interview that Sashko delivered to the online magazine *Den'* in 2017, https://day.kyiv.ua/article/podorozhi/marik.

2 Marta Studenna-Skrukwa, 'Tsartsvo vuhillia i zaliza. Rol' industrializatsii v protsesi suspil'nykh zmin na Donbasi', in *Pratsia, vysnazhennia ta uspikh: promyslovi monomista Donbasu*, ed. by Volodymyr Kulikov and Iryna Sklokina (Lviv: FOP Shumylovich, 2018), pp. 21–42 (p. 33).

3 Serhii Plokhy, 'Goodbye Lenin: A Memory Shift in Revolutionary Ukraine', *Digital Atlas of Ukraine*, Harvard University, https://gis.huri.harvard.edu/leninfall.

4 'Lenin Falls', *Digital Atlas of Ukraine*, Harvard University, https://gis.huri.harvard.edu/lenin-falls.

5 Oleksandra Gaidai, 'Leninfall in Ukraine: How Did the Lenin Statues Disappear?', *Harvard Ukrainian Studies*, 38, 1/2 (2021), pp. 45–70.

6 Oxana Shevel, 'The Battle for Historical Memory in Postrevolutionary Ukraine', *Current History*, 115, 783, Russia and Eurasia (October 2016): pp. 258–263.

7 Iryna Sklokina and Volodymyr Kulikov, 'Industrial Heritage and Its Multiple Uses in Donbas, Ukraine', *REGION: Regional Studies of Russia, Eastern Europe, and Central Asia*, 10, 1 (January 2021), (pp. 33–60) (p. 51).

8 The Ilych in question was himself a steelmaker and academic from nearby Melitopol, Zot Il'ych Nekrasov. My thanks to Andrii Prokopov for clarifying this detail.

9 Hiroaki Kuromiya, *Freedom and Terror in the Donbas: A Ukrainian-Russian Borderland, 1870s–1990s* (Cambridge: Cambridge University Press, 1998), pp. 77–86.

10 Theodore H. Friedgut, *Iuzovka and Revolution: Life and Work in Russia's Donbass, 1869–1924* (Princeton, NJ: Princeton University Press, 2014), pp. 77–8.

11 Kuromiya, *Freedom and Terror in the Donbas*, p. 94.

12 Quoted in Kuromiya, *Freedom and Terror in the Donbas*, p. 114.

13 Pshenychnyi Audio-Visual Archive, MI 3, Donetska oblast'.

14 Victoria Donovan, 'Vitannia z Iuzivki! Lystuvannia brytans'kykh migrantiv ta pryv'iazanist' do mistsia v industrial'nomu landshafti Donbasu v kin. XIX – poch. XX st.', *Histor!ans.ua*, 06 January 2020.

15 John Berger, 'The Suit and the Photograph', in *About Looking* (New York: Pantheon Books, 1980).

16 Alena V. Ledeneva, *Russia's Economy of Favours: Blat, Networking and Informal Exchange* (Cambridge: Cambridge University Press, 1998).

17 Yuliya Yurchenko, *Ukraine and the Empire of Capital: From Marketisation to Armed Conflict* (London: Pluto Press, 2018), p. 66.

18 Shaun Walker, 'With Viktor Yanukovych gone, Ukraine hunts for secrets of former leader', *Guardian*, 23 February 2014, https://www.theguardian.com/world/2014/feb/23/viktor-yanukovych-ukraine-secret-documents.

19 Kuromiya, *Freedom and Terror in the Donbas*, p. 120.

20 *Ibid.*, p. 127.

21 Marta Studenna-Skrukwa, 'Tsartsvo vuhillia i zaliza', pp. 34–5.

22 Hiroaki Kuromiya, 'The Shakhty Affair', *South East European Monitor*, 4, 2 (1997), pp. 41–64.

23 Lewis Siegelbaum, *Stakhanovism and The Politics of Productivity in the USSR, 1935–1941* (Cambridge; New York: Cambridge University Press, 1988), p. 69.

24 *Ibid.*, p. 146.

25 *Ibid.*

26 *Stakhanov* (Mosfilm, 1986). Documentary film held at the Pshenychnyi Archive in Kyiv.

27 Olena Stiazhkina and Iryna Sklokina, 'Zhyttia pislia roboty', in *Pratsia, vysnazhennia ta uspikh: promyslovi monomista Donbasu*, ed. by Volodymyr Kulikov and Iryna Sklokina (Lviv: FOP Shumylovych, 2018), pp. 131–56 (pp. 147–51).

28 '"Kessonnaia bolezn"' Alekseia Stakhanova', *BBC News Russkaia sluzhba*, 31 July 2015, https://www.bbc.com/russian/russia/2015/07/150731_ussr_stakhanov.

29 For a pre-history of Soviet 'boards of honour', see R. O. Abilova, 'Ona vsegda so mnoi': K istorii nastennogo fotoal'boma', *Vestnik Chuvashskogo universiteta*, 4 (2015), pp. 5–10 (pp. 5–6).

30 Serguei Oushakine, 'Presence Without Identification: Vicarious Photography and Postcolonial Figuration in Belarus', *October*, 164 (2018), pp. 49–88 (pp. 57–9).

31 Ol'ga Bashkirova *et al.*, *Serdtse ukrainskoi metallurgii. 120 let MMK imeni Il'icha* (Mariupol: ChAO Gazeta 'Priazovskii rabochii', 2016), p. 39.

32 'Udarnichestvo' stand at Ilych Iron and Steelmaking Museum, November 2021.

33 Iryna Sklokina has commented on the shifting focus of labour cults in different periods of Soviet rule, noting the predominance of young workers in the photography of hero workers in the 1920s photographs and the prevalence of retired men in the early 1950s, reflecting the conservative shift in late Stalinism. Iryna Sklokina, 'Fotoobrazi Donbasu: stvorennia, sotsial'ne zhittia, arkhivuvannia' in *Pratsia, vysnazhennia ta uspikh*, ed. by Kulikov and Sklokina (Lviv: FOP Shumylovych, 2018), pp. 216–17.

34 'Liudyna-legenda' stand at the Ilych Iron and Steelmaking Museum, November 2021.

35 On the 'khaziain' figure, see Denys Gorbach, 'Changing Patronage and Informality Configurations in Ukraine: From the Shop Floor Upwards', *Studies of Transition States and Societies*, 12, 1 (2020), pp. 3–15; and Denys Gorbach, 'Underground Waterlines: Explaining Political Quiescence of Ukrainian Labor Unions', *Focaal*, p. 84 (2019), pp. 33–46.

36 Bashkirova, *Serdtse ukrainskoi metallurgii*, pp. 71–2.

37 Jeffrey Brooks, *Thank You, Comrade Stalin! Soviet Popular Culture From Revolution to Cold War* (Princeton NJ: Princeton University Press, 2000).

4. BRIGHT CITY

1 The summer school 'The Plant Gave Us Everything: the role of art and community engagement in the cultural transformation of Donbas monotowns' was curated by Darya Tsymbalyuk and Dmytro Chepurnyi, in partnership with the 'Donbas Studies' programme at IZOLYATSIA: Platform for Cultural Initiatives in 2019. The summer school was supported by the Global Challenges Research Fund-funded project 'De-industrialization and Conflict in Donbas' at the University of St Andrews.

2 V. V. Butov and S.A. Pertsovskii, *Severodonetskoe proizvodstvennoe ob'edinenie 'Azot': illiustrirovannyi prospekt* (Donetsk: Donbas, 1978), p. 3.

3 Serhii Kaleniuk, Mykola Lomako, *Davnia istoriia Severodonets'ka. Mandrivka kraem za davnimy kartamy m. Severodonets'k* (Sevierodonets'k, 2009), p. 1.

4 S. P. Kaleniuk, 'Sotsialistchne misto Sieverodonets'k: proiekty i diisnist', *Slobozhanshchyna. Pohliad u mynule* (Zhytomyr: Vydavets O. O. Yevenok, 2018), p. 65.

5 *Ibid.*

6 Similar kinds of geometric planning could also be found in company towns in the United States. See Margaret Crawford, 'The "New" Company Town', *Perspecta*, 30 (1999), pp. 48–57.

7 Quoted in S. P. Kaleniuk, 'Sotsialistichne misto Sievierodonets'k: proiekty i diisnist', p. 71.

8 Brian Milakovsky, 'A frontline factory, an embattled oligarch and Ukraine's industrial drift', *openDemocracy*, 02 May 2018, https://www.opendemocracy.net/en/odr/a-frontline-factory/.

9 Following Russian missile strikes in 2022, two such chemical disasters took place, one at the Zoria Factory in Rubizhne and one at AZOT in Sievierodonetsk. Thanks to Oleksandr Kuchynskyi for this information.

10 Milakovsky, 'A frontline factory'.

11 'Letopis' komsomol'skoi organizatsii Severodonetskogo ordena Lenina Proizvodstvennogo ob'edineniia "Azot" im. Leninskogo komsomola (1951–1991 gg.)'. Online publication, formerly available on the 'AZOT' factory website (no longer accessible since the city's occupation in 2022).

12 Butov and Pertsovskii, *Severodonetskoe proizvodstvennoe ob'edinenie 'Azot'*, p. 5.

13 Svitlana Oslavs'ka, *Sievierodonets'k. Reportazhi z mynuloho* (Kyiv: Choven, 2022), p. 103.

14 Lewis Siegelbaum, *Stakhanovism and The Politics of Productivity in the USSR, 1935–1941* (Cambridge; New York: Cambridge University Press, 1988), p. 212.

15 Iryna Sklokina, 'Fotoobrazy Donbasu: stvorennia, sotsial'ne zhyttia, arkhivuvannia', in *Pratsia, vysnazhennia ta uspikh: promyslovi monomista Donbasu*, ed. by Iryna Sklokina and Volodymyr Kulikov (Lviv: FOP Shumylovych, 2018), p. 214.

16 Robert B. Hamanaka and Gökhan M. Mutlu, 'Particulate Matter Air Polution: Effects on the Cardiovascular System', *Front. Endocrinol. (Lausanne)*, 9 (2018), p. 680.

17 Oslavs'ka, *Sievierodonets'k. Reportazhi z minuloho*, pp. 103–104.

18 Butov and Pertsovskii, *Severodonetskoe proizvodstvennoe ob'edinenie 'Azot'*, p. 24.

19 'Letopis' komsomol'skoi organizatsii Severodonetskogo ordena Lenina Proizvodstvennogo ob'edineniia "Azot" im. Leninskogo komsomola (1951–1991gg.)'.

20 *Ibid.*

21 *Ibid.*

22 Sklokina, 'Fotoobrazy Donbasu', p. 214.

23 Oslavs'ka, *Sievierodonets'k. Reportazhi z mynulogo*, p. 103.

24 *Ibid.*

25 Butov and Pertsovskii, *Severodonetskoe proizvodstvennoe ob'edinenie 'Azot'*, p. 28.

26 'Letopis' komsomol'skoi organizatsii Severodonetskogo ordena Lenina Proizvodstvennogo ob'edineniia "Azot" im. Leninskogo komsomola (1951–1991gg.)'.

27 Butov and Pertsovskii, *Severodonetskkoe proizvodstvennoe ob'edinenie 'Azot'*, p. 29.

28 Aleksandr Yakubenko, Vladimir Varaksin, 'Severodonetskii ledovyi dvorets sporta', *Severodonets'k Onlain*, 10 May 2016, https://sd.ua/news/4882.

29 *Ibid.*

30 Oslavs'ka, *Sievierodonets'k. Reportazhi z mynuloho*, p. 103.

31 Yakubenko and Varaksin, 'Severodonetskii ledovyi dvorets sporta'.

32 Oslavs'ka, *Severodonets'k. Reportazhi z mynuloho*, p. 128.

33 Denys Kazans'kyi and Maryna Vorotyntseva, *Yak Ukraina vtrachala Donbas* (Kyiv: Chorna hora, 2020), pp. 95–102.

34 Yuliya Yurchenko, *Ukraine and the Empire of Capital: From Marketisation to Armed Conflict* (London: Pluto Press, 2018), pp. 83–9.

35 Brian Milakovsky, 'A frontline factory'.

36 Freefilmers, *Vy sho, tut metall voruete?* (2018), https://www.youtube.com/watch?v=dK5fGrGaMRo.

37 Evhenii Tetianychko, 'V Severodonetske vozrozhdaiut kul'tovoe kafe 'Mozaika'. Smotrite, chto seichas proiskhodit so zdaniem', *Svoi.city*, 22 June 2021, https://svoi.city/articles/150771/v-severodonecke-vozrozhdayut-kultove-kafe-mozaika.

38 Victoria Donovan and Darya Tsymbalyuk, *Limits of Collaboration: Art, Ethics, and Donbas* (Kyiv: Rosa Luxemburg Press, 2022), p. 44.

39 For more information on the UrbEx movement, see https://www.urbex.co.uk/.

40 Victoria Donovan and Darya Tsymbalyuk, 'Vid ruin porn do "zabroshka-erotyky": Doslidzhennia Viktorii Donovan ta Dar'i Tsymbaliuk pro Sievierodonets'k, *YourArt*, 08 February 2021, https://supportyourart.com/stories/vid-ruin-porn-do-zabroshka-erotyky/.

5. PINK SKIES

1 Anna Balazs, 'In-Between Futures: Urban transformation in an East Ukrainian frontline city', unpublished PhD dissertation at University of Manchester, 2020, p. 205.

2 Iryna Sklokina, 'Fotoobrazy Donbasu: stvorennia, sotsial'ne zhittia, arkhivuvannia', in *Pratsia, vysnazhennia ta uspikh: promyslovi monomista Donbasu*, ed. by Volodymyr Kulikov and Iryna Sklokina (Lviv: FOP Shumylovych, 2018), pp. 188–9.

3 See, for example, Paul Josephson *et al.*, 'Creating the Socialist Industrial, Urban, and Agricultural Environment', in *An Environmental History of Russia*, ed. Paul Josephson *et al.* (Cambridge: Cambridge University Press, 2013), pp. 71–135.

4 See V. A. Iakovenko *et al.*, 'Zagriaznenie atmosfernogo vozdukha promyshlennykh gorodov Donbassa', in *Donbass: Ego sanitarnoe izuchenie i ozdorovlenie. T.2: Gigienicheskoe izuchenie zhilishch Donbassa. Zagriaznenie vozdukha prompredpriiatiami. Ochistka rabochikh poselkov*, ed. by A. N. Marzeev (Kherson: Gos. Med. Izd-vo USSR, 1945), pp. 95–133.

5 Kate Brown, *Manual for Survival: A Chernobyl Guide to the Future* (London: Allen Lane, 2019).

6 'Ekotsyd ta ekolohichna revoliutsiia kintsia 1980-kh rokiv', *Ekolohiia u fokusi*, a digital exhibition co-curated by Anna Bahachenko, Dmytro Bilko, Victoria Donovan, Volodymyr Kulikov, and Iryna Sklokina (Lviv, 2022), https://ecology.lvivcenter.org.

7 Yelizaveta Derenova, 'Notatky pro kinoamatoriv/-ok Mariupolia u 1950-80-kh rokakh', *Mariupol's'kyi park pam'iati*, a digital archive produced by Sashko Protyah and co-edited by Nichka Lishchans'ka, Victoria Donovan, and Diána Vonnák (2023), https://www.mariupolmemorypark.space/library/kinoamatorky-mariupolia/.

8 'Kudy my idemo?' dir. by N. Chukhlib *et al.* (Mariupol, 1989), https://vimeo.com/749599630/addc9c4940.

9 'Perestroika', meaning 'restructuring', was a policy of economic reform, primarily intended to revive the stagnating socialist economy in the late 1980s.

10 Collections of photographs and newspapers were held at the Mariupol Local History Museum, which was destroyed in 2022. Parts of the collection were digitised through the 'Un/archiving Post/industry' project in 2020–21 and are available through the Center for Urban History's Urban Media Archive, https://uma.lvivcenter.org/en/photos?dates=1600%2C2024&full-search=&places%5B112%5D=138. See, also, 'Fotolitopis Mariupolia: Chastyna 1. Fotokhudozhnik Boris Dembytskyi. Fotoistoriia Mariupolia' (2021), https://www.youtube.com/watch?v=Lr_FyWv0Zl4.

11 'Khochu dishat'. YouTube (2018): hhttps://www.youtube.com/watch?v=Pkdc92GcYbo.

12 Iryna Gorbas'ova, 'My fakticheski obmanyvaem evropeitsev – Maksim Borodin o tom, kak Mariupol' peredaet dannye o vozdukhe v global'nuiu sistemu', *Radio Svoboda*, 3 November 2020, https://www.radiosvoboda.org/a/30925946.html.

13 Beth Gardiner, 'Inside a Ukrainian war zone another fight rages – for clean air', *National Geographic*, 29 November 2021, https://www.nationalgeographic.com/environment/article/inside-a-ukrainian-war-zone-another-fight-ragesfor-clean-air.

14 Amy Pelka Mucha *et al.*, 'Urinary 1-hydroxypyrene as a biomarker of PAH exposure in 3-year-old Ukrainian children', *Environmental Health Perspectives*, May 2006, pp. 603–9.

15 Patrick O'Hare, *Rubbish Belongs to the Poor: Hygenic Enclosure and the Waste Commons* (London: Pluto Press, 2022).

16 Freefilmers: http://www.freefilmers.org/en/.

17 Victoria Donovan and Darya Tsymbalyuk, 'The Politics of Watching: Documentary visions of the Ukrainian East', *Klassiki*, July 2022, https://klassiki.online/the-politics-of-watching-documentary-visions-of-the-ukrainian-east/.

18 Charlie Smart, 'How the Russian Media Spread False Claims About Ukrainian Nazis', *New York Times*, 2 July 2022, https://www.nytimes.com/interactive/2022/07/02/world/europe/ukraine-nazis-russia-media.html.

19 Maryna Shevtsova, 'Looking for Stepan Bandera: The Myth of Ukrainian Nationalism and the Russian "Special Operation"', *Central European Journal of International and Security Studies*, 16:3 (2022), pp. 132–150.

20 An Independent Legal Analysis of the Russian Federation's Breaches of the Genocide Convention in Ukraine and the Duty to Prevent (2022); New Lines Institute for Strategy and Policy and Raoul Wallenberg Centre for Human Rights, May; retrieved 18 June 2022, from https://newlinesinstitute.org/russia/an-independent-legal-analysis-of-the-russian-federations-breaches-of-the-genocide-convention-in-ukraine-and-the-duty-to-prevent/

21 Taras Fedirko and Andrea E. Pia, 'War in Ukraine – an Interview with Taras Fedirko', *Association of Social Anthropologists*, 23 March 2022, https://www.theasa.org/publications/asaonline/articles/asaonline_0111.

22 'Sea of Azov IMMA', Marine Mammal Protected Areas Task Force, https://www.marinemammalhabitat.org/wp-content/uploads/imma-factsheets/BlackSeaTurkishStraitsCaspianSea/Sea-of-Azov-BlackSeaTurkishStraitsCaspianSea.pdf.

23 R. P. Bozhko *et al.*, *Mariupol' i ego okrestnosti: vzgliad iz XXI veka* (Mariupol': Izd-vo 'Renata', 2008), p. 344.

24 These scenes are documented in a short film by Mariupol filmmaker Zoya Laktionova, *Territory of Empty Windows* (2020), available on TakFlix: https://www.takflix.com/en/films/territory-empty-windows.

25 Bozhko *et al.*, *Mariupol' i ego okrestnosti*, p. 345.

26 'Shlakovye gory i opasnye poligony v Priazov'e: kak prevratit' problemu v razvitie', *0692.com.ua: Sait goroda Mariupolia*, 25 October 2021, https://www.0629.com.ua/news/3232488/slakovye-gory-i-opasnye-poligony-v-priazove-kak-prevratit-problemu-v-razvitie-foto-infografika.

27 'Circular Building and Infrastructure: State of Play Report ECESP Leadership Group on Buildings and Infrastructure', (2021), https://shorturl.at/nwz18.

28 *Ibid.*

29 Bozhko *et al.*, *Mariupol' i ego okrestnosti*, p. 344.

30 Oleksandr Yankovs'kii, '"Na ruinakh Azovstali". Chi vdast'sia okupantam vidnovyty robotu zavodu?', *Radio Svoboda*, 25 June 2022, https://www.radiosvoboda.org/a/novyny-pryazovya-mariupol-azovstal-rosiya/31914634.html.

31 Anna Balazs, '"After Every Storm There Is A Rainbow": Visual Representations of Occupied Mariupol', 'Mariupol Memory Park', Byre World Series, Byre Theatre, St Andrews, 13 September 2023.

32 'Kak okkupanty vrut o sostoianii Azovskogo moria. Chestno o real'noi situatsii vokrug Mariupola', *0692.com.ua: Sait goroda Mariupolia*, 15 August 2023, https://www.0629.com.ua/ru/news/3644613/kak-okkupanty-vrut-o-sostoanii-azovskogo-mora-cestno-o-realnoj-situacii-vokrug-mariupola.

6. CULTURAL FRONT

1 Dmytro Chepurnyi, 'Podolaty roziednannia: suchasne mystetstvo Skhodu Ukrainy', *Medium*, 4 January 2021, https://dmytrochepurnyi.medium.com/подолати-роз'єднання-сучасне-мистецтво-сходу-україни-7336eec3f5c8.

2 Victoria Donovan and Darya Tsymbalyuk, *Limits of Collaboration: Art, Ethics, and Donbas* (Kyiv: Rosa Luxemburg Stiftung v Ukraini, 2022), p. 290.

3 The idea of the war in Ukraine as a 'proxy war' between Russia and the US, supported by some parts of the Western Left and the Global South, has been critiqued in a number of articles written since the start of the full-scale invasion. See, for example, Mila O'Sullivan, Tereza Hendl, Olga Burlyuk and Aizada Arystanbek, '(En)countering Epistemic Imperialism: A Critique of "Westsplaining" and Coloniality in Dominant Debates on Russia's Invasion of Ukraine', *Contemporary Security Policy*, 4 December 2023, https://doi.org/10.1080/13523260.2023.2288468.

4 For a brief history of Pokrovsk, see *Ugol' kamennyi, liudi zolotye*, ed. by S. I. Kramarova *et al.* (Kyiv: Nash druk, 2010), pp. 23–31.

5 On the history of this factory, see *Pobedyvshii vremia.* ed. by V. V. Makotkin *et al.* (Donetsk: izdat-vo 'Donechchina', 2004).

6 'Proekt "Muzei vidkryto na remont" distavsia do Pokrovska', *Orbita telekompaniia*, 13 October 2017, https://orbita.dn.ua/proekt-muzej-vidkrito-na-remont-distavsya-do-pokrovska.html.

7 'Un/archiving Post/industry', Center for Urban History, https://www.lvivcenter.org/en/researches/un-archiving-post-industry/.

8 These images can be viewed through the Center for Urban History's Urban Media Archive, https://uma.lvivcenter.org/uk/collections/148/photos.

9 'Profession: Photojournalist. Part 2. Monochrome' (2022), *ruïns collective*, https://www.ruins.today/profession-photojournalist-2.

10 Stanislav Aseyev, *V Izoliatsii: Esei pro Donbas* (Kyiv: Chorna hora, 2021).

11 'Tu', https://tu.org.ua.

12 Others included Art Residency +/- in Sievierodonetsk, TopPlace in Sloviansk, and Vilna Khata in Kramatorsk. For an overview of community art in the region between 2014 and 2022 see Dmytro Chepurnyi, 'Podolaty roziednannia'.

13 Feemnia, 'Read while listening to Serdiuchka', *Mariupol Memory Park*, https://www.mariupolmemorypark.space/en/library-en/read-while-listening-to-serdiuchka/.

14 'IZOLYATSIA: Platform for Cultural Initiatives', https://izolyatsia.org/en/.

15 For a more detailed discussion of IZOLYATSIA's work in the region, see IZOLYATSIA in *Skhid ukrains'koho sontsia: istorii*

Donechchyny ta Luhanshchyny pochatku XXI stolittia (Lviv: Choven, 2022), pp. 66-71.

16 Andrii Dostliev, Lia Dostlieva, 'Licking War Wounds' (2016–2021), http://dostliev.org/lickingwarwounds.html.

17 Roksolana Dudka's work in Soledar can be viewed through the drop-down menu at the bottom of the page 'Series of short term residencies *Grounding* in Soledar', IZOLYATSIA: Platform for Cultural Initiatives, https://izolyatsia.org/en/project/zazemlennya-residency.

18 Tetiana Pavliuk and Irena Tischenko, 'Soledar: Ochikuvannia i real'nist' Tetiana Paliuk ta Irena Tyshchenko pro uchast' artrezydentsii "Zazemlennia"', *YourArt*, 12 April 2021, https://supportyourart.com/stories/soledar-ochikuvannya-i-realnist-tetyana-pavlyuk-ta-irena-tyshhenko-pro-uchast-v-artrezydencziyi-zazemlennya/.

19 Emily Channell-Justice, *Without the State: Self-Organisation and Political Activism in Ukraine* (Toronto: University of Toronto Press, 2022).

20 Darya Tsymbalya and I discuss this concept in more detail in *Limits of Collaboration*, pp. 14–16.

7. BIG WAR

1 'Ukraine Situation', UNHCR: The UN Refugee Agency, https://reporting.unhcr.org/operational/situations/ukraine-situation.

2 Malaka Shwaikh, 'Beyond Expectations of Resilience: Towards a a Language of Care', *Global Studies Quarterly*, 3, 2 (April 2023), https://academic.oup.com/isagsq/article/3/2/ksad030/7198303.

3 Kateryna Iakovlenko writes about the circulation of images of corpses in wartime Ukraine in 'Exactly That Body: Images Against Oppression', *e-flux Journal*, 133 (February 2023), https://www.e-flux.com/journal/133/517485/exactly-that-body-images-against-oppression/.

4 Diána Vonnák, '"This Happened to Us for the Second Time": War-preparedness, Risk, Responsibility, and the Evacuation of Donbas Museums in 2022', *Museum & Society*, 21, 2 (2023), https://journals.le.ac.uk/ojs1/index.php/mas/article/view/4305/3750.

5 *My Favourite Job*, directed by Sashko Protyah (2022), https://www.mariupolmemorypark.space/en/cinema-en/.

6 Katerina Sergatskova, 'Twenty Two Kilometers on Foot past Russian Checkpoints: Journalist Oksana Semenyk Recounts How She Fled from Occupied Bucha', *Zaborona*, 11 March 2022, https://zaborona.com/en/journalist-oksana-semenyk-recounts-how-she-fled-from-occupied-bucha/.

7 @ukr_arthistory, https://twitter.com/ukr_arthistory.

8 Diána Vonnák, 'Heritage Preservation and the Transforming State in Lviv: A Changing Professional Field', unpublished PhD thesis, Durham University, 2020, pp. 36–60.

9 Mykhailo Kulishov, SVOI.CITY, https://svoi.city/articles/author/3573.

10 Mykhailo Kulishov, 'Palats kul'tury u Bakhmuti. Kolis' velychnyi, a teper znyshchenyi rosiianamy', SVOI.CITY, 18 August 2023, https://svoi.city/articles/305989/rozbitij-rosiyanami-palac-kulturi-u-bahmuti.

11 'Shliakh, poznachenyi silliu', a project by Mykhailo Kulishov, realised with support of IZOLYATSIA: Platform for Cultural Initiatives, https://saltway.in.ua/saltway-vr/.

Select Bibliography

Abilova, R. O., "'Ona vsegda so mnoi": K istorii nastennogo fotoal'boma', *Vestnik Chuvashskogo universiteta*, 4 (2015), pp. 5–10

Bahachenko, Anna, Dmytro Bilko, Victoria Donovan, Volodymyr Kulikov, and Iryna Sklokina, 'Ekotsyd ta ekolohichna revoliutsiia kintsia 1980-kh rokiv', *Ekolohiia u fokusi* (Lviv, 2022), https://ecology.lvivcenter.org

Balazs, Anna, 'In-Between Futures: Urban transformation in an East Ukrainian frontline city', unpublished PhD dissertation at University of Manchester, 2020

Bashkirova, Olivia, *et al.*, *Serdtse ukrainskoi metallurgii. 120 let MMK imeni Il'icha* (Mariupol': ChAO 'Gazeta 'Priazovskii rabochii, 2016)

Bazdyrieva, Asia, 'No Milk, No Love', *e-flux*, 127, May 2022, https://www.e-flux.com/journal/127/465214/no-milk-no-love/

Berger, John, *About Looking* (New York: Pantheon Books, 1980)

Bovykin, I. V., ed., *Inostrannoe predprinimatel'stvo i zagranichenye investitsii v Rossii. Ocherki* (Moscow: Rosspen, 1997)

Bozhko, R. P., T. Yu Buli, N. N. Gashenenko *et al.*, *Mariupol' i ego okrestnosti: vzgliad iz XXI veka* (Mariupol Culture: Izd-vo 'Renata', 2008)

Brooks, Jeffrey, *Thank You, Comrade Stalin! Soviet Popular Cultural From Revolution to Cold War* (Princeton NJ: Princeton University Press, 2000)

Brown, Kate, *Manual for Survival: A Chernobyl Guide to the Future* (London: Allen Lane, 2019)

Butov, V. V. and S. A. Pertsovskii, *Severodonetskoe proizvodstvennoe ob'edinenie 'Azot': illiustrirovannyi prospekt* (Donetsk: Donbas, 1978)

Channell-Justice, Emily, *Without the State: Self-Organisation and Political Activism in Ukraine* (Toronto: University of Toronto Press, 2022)

Chepurnyi, Dmytro, 'Podolaty roziednannia: suchasne mystetstvo Skhodu Ukrainy', *Medium*, 4 January 2021, https://dmytrochepurnyi.medium.com/подолати-розєднання-сучасне-мистецтво-сходу-україни-7336eec3f5c8

'Circular Building and Infrastructure: State of Play Report ECESP Leadership Group on Buildings and Infrastructure', (2021), https://shorturl.at/nwz18

Derenova, Yelizaveta, 'Notatky pro kinoamatoriv/-ok Mariupolia u 1950-80-kh rokakh', *Mariupol's'kyi park pam'iati* a digital archive produced by Sashko Protyah and co-edited by Nichka Lishchans'ka, Victoria Donovan, and Diána Vonnák (2023), https://www.mariupolmemorypark.space/library/kinoamatorky-mariupolia/

Digital Atlas of Ukraine, Harvard University, https://gis.huri.harvard.edu/leninfall

Donovan, Victoria, 'Vitannia z Iuzivki! Lystuvannia brytans'kykh migrantiv ta pryv'iazanist' do mistsia v industrial'nomu landshafti Donbasu v kin. XIX – poch. XX st.', *Histor!ans.ua*, 6 January 2020.

Donovan, Victoria, and Darya Tsymbalyuk, with Dmytro Chepurnyi, Viktor 'Corwic' Zasypk, Oleksandr Kuchynskyi, and Kateryna Siryk, *Limits of Collaboration: Art, Ethics, and Donbas* (Kyiv: Rosa Luxemburg Press, 2022)

＿＿＿, 'The Politics of Watching: Documentary visions of the Ukrainian East', *Klassiki*, July 2022, https://klassiki.online/the-politics-of-watching-documentary-visions-of-the-ukrainian-east/

_____, 'Vid ruin porn do "zabroshka-erotyky": Doslidzhennia Viktorii Donovan ta Dar'i Tsymbaliuk pro Sievierodonets'k', *YourArt*, 8 February 2021, https://supportyourart.com/stories/vid-ruin-porn-do-zabroshka-erotyky/

Durand, Olivia Irena, '"New Russia" and the Legacies of Settler Colonialism in Southern Ukraine', *Journal of Applied History*, 12 December 2022, pp. 62–3

Fedirko, Taras, and Andrea E. Pia, 'War in Ukraine – an Interview with Taras Fedirko', *Association of Social Anthropologists*, 23 March 2022, https://www.theasa.org/publications/asaonline/articles/asaonline_0111

Feemnia, 'Read while listening to Serdiuchka', *Mariupol Memory Park*, https://www.mariupolmemorypark.space/en/library-en/read-while-listening-to-serdiuchka/

Friedgut, Theodore H., *Iuzovka and Revolution: Life and Work in Russia's Donbass, 1869–1924* (Princeton, NJ: Princeton University Press, 2014)

_____, 'Labour Violence and Regime Brutality in Tsarist Russia: The Iuzovka Cholera Riots of 1892', *Slavic Review*, 46, 2 (1987)

Gaidai, Oleksandra, 'Leninfall in Ukraine: How Did the Lenin Statues Disappear?', *Harvard Ukrainian Studies*, 38, 1/2 (2021), pp. 45–70

Gardiner, Beth, 'Inside a Ukrainian war zone another fight rages – for clean air', *National Geographic*, 29 November 2021, https://www.nationalgeographic.com/environment/article/inside-a-ukrainian-war-zone-another-fight-ragesfor-clean-air

Gorbach, Denys, 'Changing Patronage and Informality Configurations in Ukraine: From the Shop Floor Upwards', *Studies of Transition States and Societies*, 12, 1 (2020), pp. 3–15

_____, 'Underground Waterlines: Explaining Political Quiescence of Ukrainian Labor Unions', *Focaal*, 84 (2019), pp. 33–46

Gorbas'ova, Iryna, 'My fakticheski obmanyvaem evropeitsev – Maksim Borodin o tom, kak Mariupol' peredaet dannye o vozdukhe v global'nuiu sistemu', *Radio Svoboda*, 3 November 2020, https://www.radiosvoboda.org/a/30925946.html

Grushevskii, D., *Imeni Il'icha: iz istorii ordena Lenina Zhdanovskogo zavoda imeni Il'icha* (Donetsk: Izd-vo 'Donbass', 1966)

Hamanaka, Robert B., and Gökhan M. Mutlu, 'Particulate Matter Air Pollution: Effects on the Cardiovascular System', *Front. Endocrinol. (Lausanne)*, 16 November 2018

Hanneke, Hariett, and Olga van den Muyzenberg, eds., trans. by S. Ovcharenko and N. Zhukova, *Stupki i gollandskaia solianaia shakhta 'Petr Velikii'. Stroeniia i te, kto zhil i rabotal tam* (Bakhmut: Stichting Van den Muyzenberg-Kiessler, 2013)

Hein-Kircher, Heidi, and Martin Zuckert, eds., *Migration and Landscape Transformation. Changes in Central and Eastern Europe in the 19th and 20th Century* (Göttingen: Vandenhoeck & Ruprecht, 2016)

Iakovlenko, Kateryna, 'Exactly That Body: Images Against Oppression', *e-flux Journal*, 133, February 2023, https://www.e-flux.com/journal/133/517485/exactly-that-body-images-against-oppression/

Josephson, Paul, *et al.*, eds., *An Environmental History of Russia* (Cambridge: Cambridge University Press, 2013)

'Kak okkupanty vrut o sostoianii Azovskogo moria. Chestno o real'noi situatsii vokrug Mariupolia', *0692.com.ua: Sait goroda Mariupolia*, 15 August 2023, https://www.0629.com.ua/ru/news/3644613/kak-okkupanty-vrut-o-sostoanii-azovskogo-mora-cestno-o-realnoj-situacii-vokrug-mariupola

Kaleniuk, Serhii, 'Sotsialistichne misto Sieverodonets'k: proiekty i diisnist'', *Slobozhanshchyna. Pohliad u mynule.* (Zhytomyr: Vydavets O. O. Yevenok, 2018)

Kaleniuk, Serhii, and Mykola Lomako, *Davnia istoriia Severodonets'ka. Mandrivka kraem za davnimy kartami m. Severodonets'k* (Sievierodonetsk, 2009)

Kazanskyi, Denys, and Marina Vorotyntseva, *Yak Ukraina vtrachala Donbas* (Kyiv: Chorna hora, 2021)

"'Kessonnaia bolezn'" Alekseia Stakhanova', *BBC News Russkaia sluzhba*, 31 July 2015, https://www.bbc.com/russian/russia/2015/07/150731_ussr_stakhanov

Khodarkovsky, Michael, *Russia's Steppe Frontier: The Making of a Colonial Empire, 1500–1800* (Bloomington, Indiana: Indiana University Press, 2004)

Kovalevskii, Evhraf Petrovich, 'Geognosticheskoe obozrenie Donetskogo gornogo kriazha', *Gornyi zhurnal* (St Petersburg: Tipografiia ekspeditsii zagotovleniia gosudarstvennykh bumag, Knizhka 1, 1829)

Kramarova, S.I., ed., *Ugol' kamennyi, liudi zolotye* (Kyiv: Nash druk, 2010)

Kulikov, Volodymyr, *Pidpriemstva i suspil'stvo v zavods'kykh i shakhtars'kykh poselenniakh Donbasu ta Pridniprov'ia v 1870–1917 rr.* (Kharkiv: Vid-vo KhHU imeni V. N. Karazina, 2019)

Kulishov, Mykhailo, 'Kovalevskii E. P. Petrograficheskaia karta Donetskogo gornogo kriazha, prostiraiushchegosia po Bakhmutskomu i Slavianoserbskomu uezdam Ekaterinoslavskoi gubernii i po Miusskomu nachal'stvu zemli Voiska Donskogo, sostavlennaia na osnovanii nabliudenii i otkrytii 1823 i 1827 godov', *Shakhty i rudnyky Donbasa*, https://www.donmining.info/2016/07/kovalevskiy-petrograficheskaya-karta-donetskogo-gornogo-kryazha.html

_____, 'Materialy kruhloho stola "Staroho rudnika"', in *Kryvoluts'ki chytannia – 2023: Mynule, vidrodzhene viinoiu. Liudy, ob'ekty, podii. Zbirnyk istoryko-kraeznavchykh prats'* (Kharkiv: Machulin, 2023), pp. 229–30

_____, 'Palats kul'tury u Bakhmuti. Kolis' velychnyi, a teper znyshchenyi rosiianamy', SVOI.CITY, 18 August 2023, https://svoi.city/articles/305989/rozbitij-rosiyanami-palac-kulturi-u-bahmuti

_____, 'Shliakh, poznachenyi silliu', https://saltway.in.ua/saltway-vr/

_____, 'Torskie ozera. Chertezh gorodam ukrainskim i cherkasskim ot Moskvy do Kryma (okolo 1670 g.)', *Shakhty i rudniki Donbassa,* https://www.donmining.info/2018/11/1670-torskie-ozera-chertezh -cherkasskim-gorodkam.html

Kulishov, M.V., O.V. Drogomirets'ka and Ya.V. Synytsia, *Shliakh, poznachenii silliu. Solona istoriia Skhodu Ukrainy* (Kramators'k: Drukars'kii dim, 2022)

Kuromiya, Hiroaki, *Freedom and Terror in the Donbas: A Ukrainian-Russian Borderland, 1870s–1990s* (Cambridge: Cambridge University Press, 1998)

_____, 'The Shakhty Affair', *South East European Monitor,* 4, 2 (1997), pp. 41–64

Laruelle, Marlene, 'The Three Colors of Novorossiya, or the Russian Nationalist Mythmaking of the Ukrainian Crisis', *Post-Soviet Affairs,* 32, 1 (2016), pp. 55–74

Lazebnyk, Valentyna, *Stal' u stepi. Pohliad z Ukraini. Istorichni narisi* (Dnipro: 'Art-Svit', 2017)

Ledeneva, Alena V., *Russia's Economy of Favours: Blat, Networking and Informal Exchange* (Cambridge: Cambridge University Press, 1998)

Levakovskii, I. O., *O slavianskikh solianykh ozerakh* (Trudy Obshchestva ispytatelei prirody pri Imperatorskom Khar'kovskom universitete, 1869, T.1.)

Limans'kyi, Serhii, *Viddilennia Ukrainsk'oho stepovoho prirodnoho zapovidnika 'Kreidova Flora'* (Ukrainian Nature Conservation Group, 2018)

Lomako, M. M., and M. V. Kulishov, 'Poshuky vugil'noi balky Skeliuvatoi v okolytsiakh Bakhmuta', *Grani istorii: zb. Nauk prats. Spetsial'nyi vypusk – materialy II Vseukrains'koi naukovo-praktichnoi konferentsii 'Bakhmuts'ka starovyna: kraeznavchi doslidzhennia'* (Slovians'k, 2018), Vip. 1(9)

Makotkin, V. V., *et al.*, *Pobedyvshiie vremia: Posviashchaetsia 70-letiiu OAO 'Krasnoarmeiskii dinasovyi zavod'* (Donetsk: izdat-vo 'Donechchina', 2004)

Marzeev, A. N., *Donbas: Ego sanitarnoe izuchenie i ozdorovlenie. T.2: Gigienicheskoe izuchenie zhilishch Donbassa. Zagriaznenie vozdukha prompredpriiatiami. Ochistka rabochikh poselkov* (Kherson: Gos. Med. Izd-vo USSR, 1945)

McKay, John P., 'Cockerill in Southern Russia, 1885–1905: A Study of Aggressive Foreign Entrepreneurship', *The Business History Review*, 41, 3 (1967)

McKay, John P., *Pioneers for Profit: Foreign Entrepreneurship and Russian Industrialization, 1885–1913* (Chicago & London: University of Chicago Press, 1970)

Mendeleev, D. I., 'Budushchaia sila, pokoiashchaiasia na beregakh Dontsa. Mirovoe znachenie kamennogo uglia i Donetskogo basseina', *Severnyi vestnik* (August–December 1888)

Milakovsky, Brian, 'A frontline factory, an embattled oligarch and Ukraine's industrial drift', *openDemocracy*, 2 May 2018, https://www.opendemocracy.net/en/odr/a-frontline-factory/

Morozov, L. P., *Mariupol' na vidovykh otkrytkakh. Illiustrirovannyi katalog, 1898–1917 g.g.* (Mariupol, 2009)

Nekrasovskii, Iu. Ia., *Ognennoe stoletie, 1897–1997* (Mariupol: PMTs MK 'Azovstal", 2009)

Ol', P. V., *Foreign Capital in Russia* (New York and London: Garland Publishing Inc., 1983)

Oslavs'ka, Svitlana, *Severodonets'k. Reportazhi z mynulogo* (Kyiv: Choven, 2022)

O'Sullivan, Mila, Tereza Hendl, Olga Burlyuk, and Aizada Arystanbek, '(En)countering Epistemic Imperialism: A Critique of "Westsplaining" and Coloniality in Dominant Debates on Russia's Invasion of Ukraine', *Contemporary Security Policy* 45, 2 (2024), pp. 171–209

Oushakine, Serguei, 'Presence Without Identification: Vicarious Photography and Postcolonial Figuration in Belarus', *October*, 164 (2018), pp. 49–88

Ovcharenko, Svetlana, ed., *Stoupky: Chetvertoe izmerenie, 1881–2018* (Kramatorsk: 'Pechatnyi dom', 2018)

Pavliuk, Tetiana, and Irena Tischenko, 'Soledar: Ochikuvannia i real'nist' Tetiana Paliuk ta Irena Tyshchenko pro uchast' artrezydentsii "Zazemlennia"', *YourArt*, 12 April 2021, https://supportyourart.com/stories/soledar-ochikuvannya-i-realnist-tetyana-pavlyuk-ta-irena-tyshhenko-pro-uchast-v-artrezydenczity-zazemlennya/

Peeters, Wim, *Stal' u stepu* (Kyiv: Belgian Embassy in Kyiv, 2010)

Pelka Mucha, Amy, *et al.*, 'Urinary 1-hydroxypyrene as a biomarker of PAH exposure in 3-year-old Ukrainian children', *Environmental Health Perspectives*, May 2006, pp. 603–9

Plokhy, Serhii, *The Gates of Europe: A History of Ukraine* (London: Penguin Books, 2016)

____, 'Goodbye Lenin: A Memory Shift in Revolutionary Ukraine', *Digital Atlas of Ukraine*, Harvard University, https://gis.huri.harvard.edu/leninfall

Podov, V. I., *Istoriia Donbassa. Donbass v XVII–XVIII vekakh* (Luhansk: Al'ma-Mater, 2004)

____, *Otkrytie Donbassa: Istoricheskii otcherk. Dokumenty* (Luhansk, 1991)

Pratt, Marie Louise, 'Arts of the Contact Zone', *Profession* (1991), pp. 33–40

Riumin, V., *Chto takoe kamennyi ugol'* (Kharkiv: VSSR, 1921)

Rybalko, Oleksandr, 'Pro nadazovs'kykh grekiv ta ikhni movi', *Mariupol's'kyi park pam'iati*, 2023, https://www.mariupolmemorypark.space/library/nadazovski-greky/

'Sea of Azov IMMA', Marine Mammal Protected Areas Task Force, https://www.marinemammalhabitat.org/wp-content/uploads/

imma-factsheets/BlackSeaTurkishStraitsCaspianSea/Sea-of
-Azov-BlackSeaTurkishStraitsCaspianSea.pdf

Sergatskova, Katerina, 'Twenty Two Kilometers on Foot past
Russian Checkpoints: Journalist Oksana Semenyk Recounts How
She Fled from Occupied Bucha', *Zaborona*, 11 March 2022, https://
zaborona.com/en/journalist-oksana-semenyk-recounts-how-she
-fled-from-occupied-bucha/

Shevtsova, Maryna, 'Looking for Stepan Bandera: The Myth of
Ukrainian Nationalism and the Russian "Special Operation"',
Central European Journal of International and Security Studies,
16:3 (2022), pp. 132–50

'Shlakovye gory i opasnye poligony v Priazov'e: kak prevratit'
problemu v razvitie', *0692.com.ua: Sait goroda Mariupolia*,
25 October 2021, https://www.0629.com.ua/news/3232488/
slakovye-gory-i-opasnye-poligony-v-priazove-kak-prevratit
-problemu-v-razvitie-foto-infografika

Shevel, Oxana, 'The Battle for Historical Memory in Post-
Revolutionary Ukraine', *Current History*, 115, 783 (2016),
pp. 258–263

Shwaikh, Malaka, 'Beyond Expectations of Resilience: Towards a
Language of Care', *Global Studies Quarterly*, 3, 2 (2023), pp. 1–13

Siegelbaum, Lewis, *Stakhanovism and The Politics of Productivity
in the USSR, 1935–1941* (Cambridge; New York: Cambridge
University Press, 1988)

Simonenko, V. D., *Ocherki o prirode Donbassa* (Donetsk: 'Donbas', 1977)

Sklokina, Iryna, 'Fotoobrazi Donbasu: stvorennia, sotsial'ne zhittia,
arkhivuvannia' in *Pratsia, vysnazhennia ta uspikh: promislovi
monomista Donbasu*, ed. by Iryna Skolkina and Volodymyr
Kulikov (Lviv: FOP Shumylovych, 2018)

Sklokina, Iryna, and Volodymyr Kulikov, 'Industrial Heritage and
Its Multiple Uses in Donbas, Ukraine', *REGION: Regional Studies
of Russia, Eastern Europe, and Central Asia*, 10, 1 (January 2021):
pp. 33–60

_____, (eds.), *Pratsia, vysnazhennia ta uspikh* (Lviv: FOP Shumylovych, 2018)

Sliusarev, A., *Priroda Donbassa: Kraevedcheskie ocherki* (Stalino: Stalinskoe oblastnoe izdatek'stvo, 1955)

Smart, Charlie, 'How the Russian Media Spread False Claims About Ukrainian Nazis', *New York Times*, 2 July 2022, https://www.nytimes.com/interactive/2022/07/02/world/europe/ukraine-nazis-russia-media.html

Stiazhkina, Olena, 'Donbas ne povernet'sia v Ukrainu, bo Donbasu ne isnue', *Ukrains'ka Pravda*, 3 November 2014, https://www.pravda.com.ua/columns/2014/11/3/7043067/

Stiazhkina, Olena, and Iryna Sklokina, 'Zhyttia pislia roboty', in *Pratsia, vysnazhennia ta uspikh: promyslovi monomista Donbasu*, ed. by Volodymyr Kulikov and Iryna Sklokina (Lviv: FOP Shumylovych, 2018), pp. 131–56

Sunderland, William, *Taming the Wild Field: Colonization and Empire on the Russian Steppe* (Ithaca: Cornell University Press, 2004)

Tetianychko, Evhenii, 'V Severodonetske vozrozhdaiut kul'tovoe kafe "Mozaika". Smotrite, chto seichas proiskhodit so zdaniem, *Svoi.city*, 22 June 2021, https://svoi.city/articles/150771/v-severodonecke-vozrozhdayut-kultove-kafe-mozaika

Tsymbalyuk, Darya, 'Erasure: Russian Imperialism, My Research on Donbas, and I', *KAJET* (2022), https://kajetjournal.com/2022/06/15/darya-tsymbalyuk-erasure-russian-imperialism-my-research-on-donbas/

_____, 'Pamiat' vuhillia', *Korydor: zhurnal pro suchasnu kul'turu*, 29 February 2020, http://korydor.in.ua/ua/stories/pam-iat-vuhillia.html

Vonnák, Diána, 'Heritage Preservation and the Transforming State in Lviv: A Changing Professional Field', unpublished PhD thesis, Durham University, 2020

_____, "'This Happened to Us for the Second Time": War-preparedness, Risk, Responsibility, and the Evacuation of Donbas Museums in 2022', *Museum & Society*, 21, 2 (2023), pp. 4–16

Walker, Shaun, 'With Viktor Yanukovych gone, Ukraine hunts for secrets of former leader', *Guardian*, 23 February 2014, https://www.theguardian.com/world/2014/feb/23/viktor-yanukovych-ukraine-secret-documents

Westwood, J. N., 'John Hughes and Russian Metallurgy', *Economic History Review*, 17, 3 (1964), pp. 564–9

Yakubenko, Aleksandr, and Vladimir Varaksin, 'Severodonetskii ledovyi dvorets sporta', *Severodonets'k Onlain*, 10 May 2016, https://sd.ua/news/4882

Yankovs'kii, Oleksandr, "'Na ruinakh Azovstali". Chi vdast'sia okupantam vidnovyty robotu zavodu?', *Radio Svoboda*, 25 June 2022, https://www.radiosvoboda.org/a/novyny-pryazovya-mariupol-azovstal-rosiya/31914634.html

Yurchenko, Yuliya, *Ukraine and the Empire of Capital: From Marketisation to Armed Conflict* (London: Pluto Press, 2018)

Zarembo, Kateryna, *Skhid ukrains'koho sontsia: istorii Donechchyny ta Luhanshchyny pochatku XXI stolittia* (Lviv: Choven, 2022)

FILMS

Chukhlib, N., *et al.*, *Kudy my idemo?* (1989)

Freefilmers, *Vy sho, tut metall voruete?* (2018)

Laktionova, Zoya, *Terytoriia pustykh vikon* (2020)

Protyah, Sashko, *My Favourite Job* (2022)

ruïns collective, *Profession: Photojournalist. Part 2. Monochrome* (2022)

Vasyanovych, Valentyn, *Atlantis* (2019)

Vertov, Dziga, *Entuziiazm: Symfoniia Donbasu* (1931)

Photo Credits

All photos author's own unless otherwise stated.

viii A trench from fighting in 2014 still visible through the steppe grass at the Regional Landscape Park 'Kleban-Byk' near Kostiantynivka. 2021.

xi Ascending a slagheap at dusk in Myrnohrad. 2021.

1 Swallows flying above a sinkhole in a gypsum mine in Ivanhrad. 2021.

7 Mykola Skuridin in front of a coalseam at 'Fox Beam' in Lysychansk. 2019.

12 Mykhailo (Misha) Kulishov descending Bilokuzmynivka. 2021.

15 Calcified trees on the salt marshes of Striapivka near Soledar. 2021.

18 Flooded depths of a gypsum mine near Striapivka on the outskirts of Soledar. 2021.

22 Marsh samphire growing on the salt marshes to the south to the village of Oleksandro-Kalynove. 2021.

25 Chandelier hanging from the ceiling of a salt chapel inside the Salt Mine No. 1 in Soledar. 2021.

30 Nestor and the diretor walk through the 'Central' Mine in Toretsk. 2021.

32 Svitlana at the Skelevata Beam in Toretsk. 2021.

35 Ruins of the Azovmash plant, formerly Providence factory, in Mariupol. 2021.

40 'Glenboig' brick at the Azovmash plant in Mariupol. 2021.

42 Misha holds a spurge hawkmoth on the steppe. 2021.

45 A man cycles past a mural of a black-winged stilt and marsh samphire in Sloviansk. 2021.

50 Late afternoon in Mariupol. 2021.

52 Bullock train hauling a boiler near Hughesovka, 1910. Percy Cartwright. Photo reproduced with permission of the Glamorgan Archives, Cardiff.

57 Andrii at the Azovmash plant in Mariupol. 2021.

60 Pile of bricks at the Azovmash plant in Mariupol. 2021.

65 The Lenin monument at Yenakiieve Metallurgy Works in the Donetsk region. 1955. Photo reproduced with the permission of the Pshenychnyi Audio-Visual Archive in Kyiv.

73 Painting and a bust of Lenin at Andrii Taraman's museum in Oleksandro-Kalynove. 2021.

77 A group of workers at the Yenakiieve Metallurgy Plant in front of a blast furnace and a group of technical specialists seated around a model blast furnace. Reproduced from the album *The Launch of the Yenakiieve Plant (1924–1925)*. Reproduced with the permission of the Pshenychnyi Audio-Visual Archive in Kyiv.

81 Stakhanovite from the 'Lenin's Way' and 'Red Fighter' collective farms near Kostiantynivka. 1937 and 1938. Reproduced with the permission of the Pshenychnyi Audio-Visual Archive in Kyiv.

85 Entrance sign for the Ilych Iron and Steelmaking Plant in Mariupol. 2021.

88 Bust of Makar Mazai at the the Ilych Iron and Steelmaking Museum in Mariupol. 2021.

90 Entrance hall of the Ilych Iron and Steelmaking Plant Museum in Mariupol. 2021.

93 Portrait of Volodymyr Boiko being gifted to the the Ilych Iron and Steelmaking Plant Museum in Mariupol. 2021.

97 Dancer at the 'TerraFox' rave in Sievierodonetsk. 2019. Photo by Wojciech Siegien. Reproduced with permission of author.

102 Shadows against the wall of the hangar during the 'Terrafox' rave. 2019. Photo by Wojciech Siegien. Reproduced with permission of author.

106 Apartment building in Sievierodonetsk. 2019. Photo by Darya Tsymbalyuk. Reproduced with permission of author.

110 ZHEK-art folk sculpture of a swan made from tyres in a garden in Sievierodonetsk. 2019. Photo by Leo Trotsenko. Reproduced with permission of author.

112 Monkey bars in a yard in Sievierodonetsk. 2019.

115 Circular metal frames in front of Sievierodonetsk's Palace of Chemists. 2019. Photo by Spurgeon Vasanthakumar. Reproduced with permission of author.

117 Mosaic of ice-skaters on the Ice Palace in Sievierodonetsk. 2019. Photo by Darya Tsymbalyuk. Reproduced with permission of author.

121 Explorers looking around the ruins of Café Mosaic in Sievierodonetsk. 2019. Photo by Darya Tsymbalyuk. Reproduced with permission of author.

124 Katia Syrik at Shakhmatnoe community centre in Sievierodonetsk. 2019. Photo by Wojciech Siegien. Reproduced with permission of author.

127 Our group on top of an abandoned building in Sievierodonetsk. 2019.

129 Mariupol at sunset. 2021. Photo by Artem Bereznev. Reproduced with permission of author.

135 View of Mariupol city centre from the top of the watertower. 2021.

138 A protest rally in the center of Mariupol, late 1980s. Photo by Boris Dembitsky. Reproduced with permission of the Center for Urban History, Lviv.

141 View of the Azov Sea from City Park, Mariupol. 2021.

143 One of Artem Bereznev's biotopes in Mariupol. 2021. Photo by Artem Bereznev. Reproduced with permission of author.

145 Azovstal viewed from the other side of the river. 2021.

147 Nightime view of the factories in Mariupol. 2021. Photo by Artem Bereznev. Reproduced with permission of author.

153 Face-the-hole photograph board outside 'Nash Kutochok' café in Mariupol. 2021.

157　View of the Azov Sea, Mariupol. 2021.

161　Legs of a mannequin in the bathroom of Platforma TU in Mariupol. 2021.

172　Sunlight on apartment buildings in Pokrovsk. 2021.

174　Explorers climb the bricked-up water tower in Pokrovsk. 2021.

176　Close-up of a wall in a gypsum mine near Striapivka on the outskirts of Soledar. 2021.

181　Ukrainian-language wall art on the interior of Platforma TU in Mariupol. 2021.

186　Empty poster board for sporting events in the park in Soledar. 2021.

188　'Not Everything Is So Simple' wall art on the exterior of Radio Dja recording studio, Soledar. 2021.

191　A headdress woven from dandilions on a central reservation on the border between Poland and Ukraine. 2023.

197　Passengers and cars waiting at the border between Poland and Ukraine. 2023.

201　A tree in the memorial garden of the memorial complex for the Heavenly Hundred in Lviv. 2023.

203　Author's feet while sheltering in the cellar of a museum in Lviv. 2023.

209　Disgraced monuments resting against the wall of the yard in the Territory of Terror Museum in Lviv. 2023.

212　Lviv historic city centre. 2023.

215　Sandbags in front of the cellar windows of a building in Lviv. 2022.

226　Shadows on Skelevata Beam in Toretsk. 2021.

Index